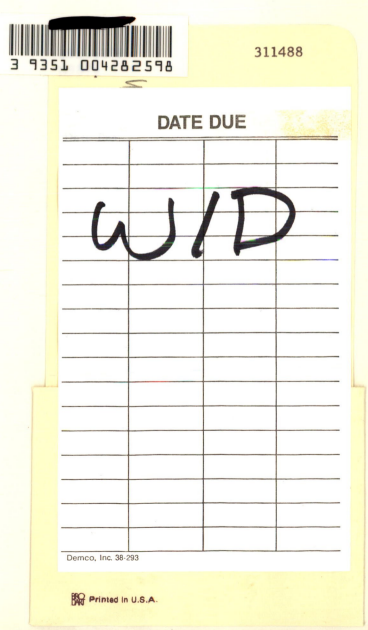

DATE DUE

W/D

Demco, Inc. 38-293

THE PASSION
BY S. MUSHAKOJI
AND
THREE OTHER JAPANESE PLAYS

THE PASSION

BY

S. MUSHAKOJI

AND

THREE OTHER JAPANESE PLAYS

TRANSLATED BY NOBORU HIDAKA

WITH AN INTRODUCTION BY

PROF. GREGG M. SINCLAIR

UNIVERSITY OF HAWAII

GREENWOOD PRESS, PUBLISHERS
WESTPORT, CONNECTICUT

Originally published in 1933
by Oriental Literature Society, University
of Hawaii, Honolulu

First Greenwood Reprinting 1971

Library of Congress Catalogue Card Number 77-98859

ISBN 0-8371-3130-8

Printed in the United States of America

CONTENTS

INTRODUCTION

Since its founding in 1596 on the dry bed of the Kamo River in Kyoto, the Kabuki, or popular theatre, has occupied an important place in the amusement life of the Japanese people. Its two historic rivals, the Noh Dance and the Marionette Theatre, have always appealed and do still appeal to special groups of spectators. The great creative period of the Noh was over long before the end of the sixteenth century; Kwanami Kiotsugu and his son, Seami,—the geniuses of the Noh,—had been dead for more than a hundred and fifty years, and no one had carried on their work in a creative way. The Doll or Marionette Theatre had made a name for itself early in the sixteenth century; and it was to exercise a marked influence on the popular drama for some time to come. Chikamatsu, for example, wrote many plays for the Doll Theatre. Yet these two forms of entertainment were more influential than popular; it was the Kabuki that appealed greatly to the Japanese people.

The Kabuki has had an interesting history,— a history, however, that tradition has somewhat encrusted. Kwanami and Seami had inculcated certain Buddhist lessons in several Noh dances, and it was these that O-Kuni is said to have portrayed at first. She may or may not have been a priestess of the celebrated Shinto Shrine of Izumo (at that time under the control of a Buddhist), but tradition has it that she arrived in Kyoto for the purpose of collecting alms for the Shrine. She danced in stately style and sang a Buddhist song or a lesson from a sutra, and enjoyed a mild success. But when Sansaburo Nagoya, a young samurai, saw her, fell in love with her, and married her, she thought of other things than Buddhist sutras. Or so at least one story out of many informs us. Sansaburo became an actor, too, arranged his wife's dances and songs to move to the popular taste—one authority tells us that he tempered the stately Noh with a little *kiogen*, or comic interlude—and soon had all Kyoto, a goodly city of a half million people, flocking to see her. So popular did she become that *daimyos* in distant provinces asked her to dance in their castles, and even the *Shogun* is said to have commanded her to perform for him.

Her great appeal, however, was to the people, and her work formed the beginning of the popular theatre in Japan, the celebrated Kabuki drama. She was an original in a new art. With the years the Kabuki has refined its art until today it is one of the achievements of the human race. The Kabuki drama is still called the popular drama, though the plays in the new dramatic style and the movies are drawing many people away.

One need not know much about the Kabuki theatre to read the four plays in this volume. They are not " Kabuki." But the more one knows of the popular theatre the more one appreciates the changes in mental approach of the modern dramatist, and how significantly these changes reveal the character of the life of today. Even as Japan has been influenced markedly by the West, so, too, have the Japanese writers been affected. The great Meiji sent commission after commission abroad to find out and to bring back the best that the Occident had to offer. Not only in matters of government, army, navy, education, banks, railways, etc., did the Itos and the Fukuzawas express themselves; they were the means of stirring the people to new activity in literature. From 1870 on, Japan was in a state of translation as well as transition. A little later—in the eighties—Dr. Tsubouchi began his great work of translating from the English, and in the nineties, Dr. Ogai Mori began to translate from the German. These two great men and their followers, by showing the people what the writers of the West were thinking of—what their beliefs were as expressed in their conduct and character—had a profound influence on Japanese life. And the Japanese novelist and playwright, writing now in a new intellectual environment, began to write differently; and the difference is patent to anyone who will read the plays in this volume. The foreign influences in them are as marked as the foreign style architecture in Tokyo is to the tourist. Yet the thought in each play is Japanese, however much it may also be foreign.

Only one of the four, *Living Koheiji*, is in the old manner, and perhaps its time setting may account for that. It is on the eternal triangle theme. Mr. Kishida's *The Roof Garden*, which contrasts the philosophy of one husband and wife with that of another husband and wife—a gleam or two of the hardness of life showing through—has several counterparts on the Occidental stage. *The Passion* indicates distinctly, I think, the influence that such writers as Strindberg have had on Japanese drama, an influence that has expressed itself in the novel, too. Mr. Mushakoji's play is not pleasant, but it is powerful, with a dramatic situation that brings out clearly the personality of each participant. Mr. Kikuchi's *The Savior of the Moment* shows a facet of Japanese character that is often overlooked, its humor. The play *is* humorous.

As played by the great Sawada in 1925 or in
1926, I thought it one of the most amusing plays
I had seen ; twice since then I have seen it on
the Occidental stage, and I am glad to say that
the humor carried over.

The four plays have been well chosen, and
Mr. Hidaka has done the difficult work of translation in exemplary style. The drama being what
it is, the direct expression of the people's thoughts,
attitudes, hopes, ambitions, we need to have more
translations of Japanese plays into English. The
present book is a welcome addition to *Orientalia*.

GREGG M. SINCLAIR,
Associate Professor, The University of Hawaii.

Honolulu, December 15, 1932.

TRANSLATOR'S NOTE

The four plays here represent a purely personal selection. Perhaps not everyone agrees, but I am convinced that they are the best works of four of Japan's leading dramatists.

Kunio Kishida, the author of *The Roof Garden*, was born in Yotsuya, Tokyo, in 1890. In his early days he began a military career, but in 1915 he decidedly gave up his military post for his literary interests, and the next year entered the Department of Literature of the Tokyo Imperial University as a special student. Later he went over to France, and took up drama as his special study. He learned dramatic arts under such great theatre-masters as Georges Pietoff, and Jacques Copeau at the " Vieux Colombier ". He returned to Japan in 1923, and immediately he began writing his unique inimitable light comedies, which are the first of the kind in Japan. Unlike comedies previously existent in Japan, his contain language colloquial yet refined, up-to-date and smart. He is a master who cleverly interweaves pathos and humor. The most pronounced in his plays is the influence by European dramatists such as Vildrac,

Romain, Molnar, and other French playwrights.

Kishida is one of the freshest, most modern-istic, dramatists of today in Japan. *The Roof Garden* is just a sketch of modern life in Tokyo, done in light touches with perfect absence of that affectation so common to modern writers. Though it is a sketch, we can feel in it an awakening of class struggle between *proletariats* and *bourgeoisie*, which is undermining Japan at present. But he had least intention to expound so called "prole-tariat-ideology", the favorite doctrine of proletariat-writers. So we can feel quite at home with this play. Those who are fond of Susan Glaspell and Ferenz Molnar will probably like this short piece.

Sensaburo Suzuki, the author of *Living Koheiji*, was born in Aoyama, Tokyo, in May, 1893. He was graduated from the night school of the Okura Commercial School, and from Koku-min Eigakukai. In 1914, he was employed in the Kyodo Fire Insurance Company, but in 1917 he resigned from the company to lead a writer's life. He wrote not a few sensational, forceful, and realistic plays. Evidently being a great follower of Strindberg, he is dauntless and bold in his material as well as in his technique. He has also written a sadistic play, *Burning Her Alive*, which has been translated by Yozan Iwasaki into English. Constructively considered, this play is superbly done, with perfect effects of climax, suspense, and anti-climax. Though it is not long, the author has made the best of it.

Living Koheiji was first presented by Kikugoro, Kanya, and Taganojo at the Shinbashi Enbujo, Tokyo, in 1925. Ochika in this play represents a new type of woman quite different from those who had been bound to home and enslaved by men for ages in feudalistic Japan.

Suzuki died on October 6, 1924, at Oiso.

Kwan Kikuchi, the author of the *The Savior of the Moment,* is, largely through Glenn Shaw's translations, one of the best known Japanese writers abroad. Kikuchi is very popular and often is called the Sinclair Lewis of Japan. Though his popularity depends on his novels, he is more of a dramatist than a novelist. His plays are well constructed and clever. He has written excellent one-act plays, such as *Father Returns, The Miracle, Tojuro's Love,* and many others.

The Savior of the Moment is a good farce, highly entertaining and a bit moralistic.

Saneatsu Mushakoji, the author of *The Passion,* was born in Yotsuya, Tokyo, on May 12, 1895. He was very much influenced by reading Tolstoi's works in his youth. He was on the editing staff when the " Shirakamba " magazine—famous partly because it first introduced William Blake's name in

Japan—was published.   He is also widely known as a founder of *Atarashii mura* ("a *new* village ") in Miyazaki.

Mushakoji is more of a philosopher than a dramatist ; and his essays, novels, and plays all reflect his deep thought, philisophy, and religion. *The Passion*, which I think one of his best plays, was staged by the Tsukiji Players several years ago.   It is easily noticed that the form of this play is more or less loose and careless, and has very few stage directions.   Still, it remains a forceful, realistic drama, with magnificent characterization.

The Savior of the Moment has been formerly translated as *Peacemaker* by Prof. Kunitomo and his students, and it was put on the stage by the Wakaba-kai members last year.   In translating it, I largely followed Mr. Kunitomo's translation, and tried to be a bit more faithful to the original.

I am greatly indebted to Mr. Thomas B. Clark for reading my MSS., and to Prof. Gregg M. Sinclair for writing an introduction for this book.

A.N.H.

Honolulu, December, 1932.

THE ROOF GARDEN

BY KUNIO KISHIDA

A DRAMA IN ONE ACT

"THE ROOF GARDEN"

A DRAMA IN ONE ACT

By **Kunio Kishida**

Translated by **Noboru Hidaka**

Characters : *Namiki*, a poor man
Mrs. Namiki
Miwa, a wealthy man
Mrs. Miwa

Place : The roof garden of a department-store.

Time : An afternoon about the middle of September.

[*Two couples are seen conversing. One couple belongs to the leisure class and the other to the salaried class.*

The men are talking and seem quite intimate. The women, finding it hard to break the ice, keep up a brave attempt at smiling.]

Miwa : Well, are you through with your shopping ?

Namiki : Shopping ? Why, I don't care about

that.

Miwa: Come here often?

Namiki: Yes, quite often. But rarely do I buy anything. Say, if it weren't for the roof garden, it would be no place for us.

Miwa: We don't come here very often either. Do you remember reading in the newspapers about a man who committed suicide sometime ago by jumping from this place? I was thinking of that, so I felt like coming here today.

Namiki: Oh?

[*All look down as if impressed.*]

Mrs. Miwa: Heavens! It would be terrible to jump from here.

Mrs. Namiki: Really!

Namiki: He did it because he was caught shop-lifting. Indeed, it must be one way of living.

Mrs. Miwa: What? You mean that to die is one way of living?

Miwa: Why, sure. However, it's the first time I've ever been up to a place like this, and it's quite different.

Namiki: Nowadays I don't see anything particularly that pleases me when I walk the streets, but I have made it a daily habit to come up here.

Miwa: It's just like you.

Namiki: Yes, that's so.

Miwa: I don't exactly mean that......but......

say, Mrs. Namiki, since it's been a long time since I've met Namiki and since it's the first time I've known you, let's have dinner together.

Mrs. Miwa: It's all right with me.

Miwa: I know that. [*To* Mrs. NAMIKI.] It's all right on your part too, I hope?

Mrs. Namiki [*looking at her husband*]: But ....er.........

Namiki: Well.........

Miwa: Oh, it's all right, isn't it?

Mrs. Namiki: But......I......I couldn't. Not this way. [*Looks at her dress.*]

Mrs. Miwa: Why, just look at me.

Miwa: Don't worry about clothes. I'll take you to a quiet nook where we can feel at home.

Namiki: But......but, we......er......

Miwa: Oh! Come on. Leave it up to me. [*Turning to his wife.*] Now, if you have anything to get, finish it in a jiffy, will you? I'll stay here and chat with Namiki for a while. [*Mrs.* MIWA *whispers something to her husband.*] Why, naturally so.

Namiki: Didn't you say you had to look for some things also? Go and look for them now. [*This time* Mrs. NAMIKI *whispers something to her husband.*] Why worry about such a thing?

[*The ladies go out, looking at each other and laughing.*]

Miwa: Surely, you have a cute wife.

Namiki: You took the very words out of my
mouth. I was about to say the same thing. It's
your wife who's so nice-looking. It seems as if
I'd seen her somewhere before. Ah! I wonder if
it were a frontispiece of a magazine.

Miwa: Sorry, she doesn't belong to that class.
But how about children? Have you any?

Namiki: Quite to the point, eh? Unfortu-
nately it's to be a second one.

Miwa: To be the second one, why.........?
[NAMIKI *grins bashfully*.] Oh, I'm sorry. Didn't
realize it.

Namiki: That doesn't matter, but you always
seem young. Are you happy?

Miwa: Well, I don't say I am unhappy, but
I'm not quite successful. [*pause*] Quite a stupid
story, but you are at present.........?

Namiki: You mean, my residence?

Miwa: Yes, I was coming to that, but tell me
first what you are doing at present.

Namiki: Doing? I can't do anything in
particular.

Miwa: I heard that you were writing something after you were graduated from school.

Namiki: At least I was doing something then.
Right now, why, I am having hard time getting
work.

Miwa: Why, that couldn't be.

[*A long pause.*]

Namiki [*as if an idea had struck him suddenly*]: Indeed this place is interesting. Just look at that over there, will you? What you see there is the Imperial Hotel. I've never spent even a night in one of its rooms, but when I come up here and look down on it,......I begin to feel, "Well, what about the Imperial Hotel?" Look over there. That's the Bank of Japan. Undoubtedly there's a large safe there, but such a safe is only as good as a dust pan. Not because I hate to be the loser, no, but when one is up here the reality does not register upon the sense of sight as such, but rather takes the form of a sort of caricature.

Miwa: Why do you say such a thing?

Namiki: And just look at that automobile! I've never been in a taxi except twice in my life. Once when I went to see the president off at Tokyo Station, and I was asked to hurry back for his seal which he had forgotten, and he ordered a *Jitsuyo* taxi for me then. A second time was when a friend of the president was a candidate for the Municipal Assembly and I was sent to help in the election campaign, I wondered what I was to do. But much to my amazement, I found it was to distribute leaflets by the car.

Miwa : Really, you did a thing like that, too ?

Namiki : Why, sure, I did. Look at that automobile there ! I think an automobile is a monster, that generally splashes mud on us as he passes by. But when you look at it from here, it certainly is an innocent-looking toy. It's such a clumsy and hurry-scurry kind of thing. In spite of that awkwardness it is a pretentious and nervous thing. Isn't it really a lovable animal ?

Miwa : You mentioned a president a moment ago. Are you employed in some company ?

Namiki : Not exactly a company ; just a small bookseller's. But since it has the word " company " printed over its doors, only among ourselves do we have such distinctions as president and employees. Just that.

Miwa : A bookseller's ? That would mean publication ?

Namiki : Well, that's about it.

Miwa : It must be interesting.

Namiki : Far from being so. And when I stand here, I feel a very beautiful world under my feet. Of course I don't mean that there is a display of luxurious *kimonos* and expensive accessories, but, you know, whenever I come up here I get a sense of direction. That doesn't explain itself, but what do you think is displayed directly through five stories right beneath me where I am now standing ?

[MIWA *does not answer.*] To begin with, there are feather coverlets on the ground floor. On the second floor there are beautiful long mirrors. On the third floor are *hitoe-obis*, and on the fourth ....well, I'll quit here. Anyway all these are things beyond our reach, but when I feel that I am standing on all of them, instead of having them displayed before my eyes, it somehow gives me a gay feeling entirely free from a desire to possess. Funny, isn't it? My wife seems to feel practically the same.

Miwa: That might be so. In other words it's what we call an unresticted spirit.

Namiki: I don't know what kind of spirit it is, but it's convenient. Take for instance the *obi*. Ever since last summer she has been begging me to get one for her, but I can't afford it. But women are certainly fools. She says it's enough just to look at them, just to go window-shopping. That's why we came here, and that's the end of the *obi* story. She hasn't bought it yet and this summer is nearly over. Still with a bright, happy face she criticizes the clothes of other women.

Miwa: A fine point, rather.

Namiki: I wonder if it is! [*Indicating the front with his chin.*] Look here, do you know that couple?

Miwa: I don't know them.

Namiki: That's the son of Marquis Omura, well known for his hobby of photography.

Miwa: Oh, I see. His wife, is it?

Namiki: Attractive, isn't she?

Miwa: In attractiveness, she cannot be compared with your wife.

Namiki: Oh, don't try comfort me. Even I know the value of women. By the way, do you still live with your father?

Miwa: Oh, no. We're separate now, but we're close by. Come over to our place sometime, won't you?

Namiki: Thank you, but right at present it's sort of hard to go. I can't keep up the same acquaintances I had in the old times.

Miwa: Oh, nonsense! I haven't changed any.

Namiki: It's no use......I've changed. I'm just as poor as before, but when I get out into the world I realize my position in society.

Miwa: You shouldn't feel small. For that matter, I'm a devil-may-care fellow.

Namiki: Really?

Miwa: Maybe it will be too personal, but tell me if you don't mind whether there is any future in your present position?

Namiki: My work? Why, eating is the only work I have, and nothing else.

Miwa: But you're writing something, aren't you?

Namiki: I've quit. When I know no one's going to read it, what's the use of writing trash so diligently and steadily? Of course I used to have dreams of becoming a great author, and there used to be people who flattered me, you know. It's a funny thing! You people might not understand it, but in such a society there's a large number of those who patiently wait with the hope that tomorrow may bring good luck, as a tree-frog might wait for the rain on the branch of a tree. I was one of them. But at that, trying not to break down my trust in my own strength, I put on a face as if I could find some merit at least in other people's writings. That's the reason why people of that society try to uphold each other. However, in the long run, one will get tired, and the others will be tired, too. And even when they meet they will evade the subject of personal matters. That's all. It's as if they have come back after seeing the displays in the stores or in the show-windows.

Miwa: I'm in the same boat. I haven't done anything that could really be called work.

Namiki: Well, that's a different story. However, I'm not regretting the fact at this time. I'm settled where I was destined to be placed, that is, apparently the very bottom, but for my part, I believe I'm in a very high position. [MIWA *keeps silent*.] And it really doesn't mean that I'm standing aloof from the world, but only that I've resolved I won't bustle about so much.

Miwa: In other words, you've reached the borders of perfect knowledge.

Namiki: Yes, if exaggerated. But you are staring at my hat?

Miwa: Oh, no fooling. I'm not looking at it.

Namiki: You can look at it. This hat is of course old. It wasn't purchased this year, but these days I don't care for appearances so much that I feel ashamed to wear it.

Miwa: It's all right, isn't it? That excuse of yours isn't at all like you. I'm very happy to have you talk to me so confidentially, but you don't have to do such bragging.

Namiki: I'm not bragging.

Miwa: Well, what is it if not bragging? Of course you're not trying to humiliate yourself? You know, Mr. Namiki, I......

Namiki: Oh, leave out the Mr. Just call me Namiki as in old times.

Miwa: Why do you stick to such trifles so much? Namiki, I hate to say this after not having met you for such a long time, but as you yourself have said, you have changed considerably. The changing is all right, but why do you have to assume such an attitude? You don't have to be ashamed of being poor, and you don't have to announce the fact to the world. It's quite a fad nowadays to boast about being poor, but I can tell that you are poor even if you don't say so. [NAMIKI *looks up to* MIWA's *face*; *his eyes shine strangely.*] Do you feel insulted? I'm not yet so hungry for pleasures as to feel happy by insulting others. If you have anything to say, say it. There must be a reason as to why in the course of time we were estranged from each other. At least on my part, I think I've shown you constant friendship.

Namiki: Please don't talk so loud.

Miwa: Why shouldn't I? You don't seem to hear the voice of my heart.

Namiki: I certainly have heard it.

Miwa: What! You heard it? Well then, you're having dinner with us, aren't you?

Namiki: Oh, yes. [*There are tears in his eyes.*]

[*A long pause.*]

Miwa: Perhaps your idea that a rich man is a sinner has not changed, but surely you aren't carrying the idea to such an extreme that you treat an old friend of yours like an enemy, do you?

[*pause*] Even at that, I can't be considered in the rich man's group. [*long pause*] What's the matter? You have no enthusiasm. It's no use being so downcast. By the way, are you quite healthy?

Namiki: Fortunately, yes......

Miwa: That's fine, isn't it? In that respect I'm miserable. I'm always in bed.

Namiki: Is it neuralgia?

Miwa: Yes, that, and the usual......a......a...

Namiki: Oh, is it still bad?

Miwa: It's getting worse and worse each day.

Namiki: You don't look it, though.

Miwa: That's what makes it worse. [*pause*]

Namiki: Shall we go down?

Miwa: It will be a bother if they come in after we get out, so let's wait here for a while longer. Sit down. [*They sit down.*]

Namiki: Say, Miwa, it's been ages since we met and it seems a bit too impudent of me to ask you right now, but can I borrow, let's say, about thirty yen, if your circumstances allow it?

Miwa [*for a minute staring into the face of his friend disagreeably, but immediately reaching for his purse*]: Why, certainly, I'm sure I can spare that much. [*Pulls out some bills from his wallet and hands them to* NAMIKI.]

Namiki: Thank you. [*Puts money away.*]
[*A cumbrous silence ensues.*]
Miwa: There is no wind now.
Namiki: I haven't hurt your feelings, have I?

Miwa: You're the one that's worried over such a trifle. In fact I am glad that I met you today. I'm happy that the two of us can talk to each other as in the good old days.
Namiki: A bit disappointed, eh?
Miwa: If you talk that way, then I shall feel disappointed.
Namiki: Well, maybe. After all, I'm so dumb. [*Taking out the money from his sleeve which he had just borrowed.*] You've been very kind, but I'm returning this. I don't think I like to borrow it. I'm sorry, but......
Miwa: What are you saying? You can pay me anytime you want to. Surely you want to buy something today, don't you? I suppose you are a little short of money. I'm in a fix like that myself, too, sometimes. On such an occasion we wish to be lucky enough to meet someone we know, but we rarely do. You were just lucky, today. That's all, isn't it?
Namiki: But such ideas don't occur to me.
Miwa: Anyway it's all right. Keep the money. I won't need it right away, so don't

worry about returning it so quickly.

Namiki [*grinning unpleasantly*]: To tell you the truth, I was thinking of buying my wife a *Hitoe-obi*.

Miwa [*laughing generously*]: Your wife is a lucky person. I have a little spare money right now and since it's a bit too late for a wedding gift, let me make a present to your wife to commemorate the renewal of our old friendship. In turn, with the money I just loaned you, I wish you would get something for my wife.

Namiki: I'm much obliged, but it will make things worse for me. I've said some unnecessary things and I can't take them back, but excuse me, I will do anything but that. I've made a mistake today, and I've never met a more agonizing situation for a long time. I thought man lived in this world by inertia, but I did not know that a man who revolts could be so bewildered when he hits something which doesn't resist him. What I said a while ago was all a lie that my rebellious spirit forced me to tell. I suppose you are the sort who would realize such a thing. If we had parted after I had made such a *faux-pas*, I don't think I'd ever sleep well.

Miwa: Oh, come on there, don't go back on yourself so much. Will you let me be conceited enough to think that there must be something good in myself, too, to have you ever ask me for a loan when you seem to have so much self-respect? Let's decide the matter before the wives come back.

Namiki: No, I would refuse that. I certainly would refuse it today. Take this back, too. I will start everything over again. Let's meet again five years hence. I might be more of a man, then.

Miwa: As usual, you're stubborn, aren't you? Well, do it to your satisfaction. [*Takes the money.*]

[Mrs. MIWA *and* Mrs. NAMIKI *return together.*]

Mrs. Miwa: Did you wait for a long time? There wasn't a satisfactory pattern. I had Mrs. Namiki look also, but our tastes are so entirely different.

Namiki: Well, she doesn't have very good taste.

Mrs. Miwa: Oh, no, that's not it. [*Giving a quick glance to her husband.*] My taste is rather *chic*, you know. And Mrs. Namiki has a refined taste......

Mrs. Namiki: Oh, my! not a refined taste.....

Miwa: Yes, it looks that way, and is that why you quit shopping?

Mrs. Miwa: We finally decided anyway, but I don't know whether you'll like it. I'd like to

have you look at it once.......Oh, well, no bother.
If it isn't satisfactory, I'll get it changed. You will
look at it at home, dear? Then we looked at
hitoe-obis together, for Mrs. Namiki wanted to see
them, you see, and there were some which were
very becoming to her. [*Turning to* Mrs. NAMIKI.]
Why didn't you decide on that one?

Miwa : She doesn't decide things by herself
as you do.

Mrs. Miwa : My, but......

Miwa : Now, let's go. You are all through,
aren't you? Well then, let me see......[*To his
wife.*] Where shall we go?

Namiki : Ah, as we are to call on somebody,
we want to be excused today. [*To* Mrs. MIWA.]
Thank you so much, but let's make it another
time. I'm really sorry.

Mrs. Miwa : Why, please don't say such a
thing. It's all right, isn't it, Mrs. Namiki?

Namiki : I've just remembered it. I'm very
sorry. Please excuse us today.

Miwa : If that's the case, we had better not
force them to stay. Then some day soon.

[Mrs. NAMIKI *bows in silence.*]

Mrs. Miwa : But it's terribly disappointing
......Although it's a homely place, you'll come to
call on us soon......and the two of you, remember.

Miwa : Good-bye.

[*Exeunt* Mr. *and* Mrs. MIWA.]

Mrs. Namiki: What's the matter?

Namiki: Nothing. Did you find a chemise-sleeve?

Mrs. Namiki: Why, of course, but it was so hard. I tried to buy a cheap one, but Mrs. Miwa would say, " These are much better," and choose the costly ones. [NAMIKI *is silent.*] It seems that those people have quite a lot of money. [NAMIKI *keeps quiet.*] She bought a swell *kinsha*-silk.

Namiki: And what's a *kinsha*-silk, anyway?

Mrs. Namiki: There you're at it again. [*pause*] Whom are we going to call on......now? [NAMIKI *does not answer.*] You know, *hitoe-obis* are down considerably now......wonder if we can't afford it?

Namiki: But there are very few people wearing that type of *obi* now, aren't there? Mrs. Miwa, too,......

Mrs. Namiki: No, hers is an *obi* of silk gauze.

Namiki: And what about an *obi* of silk gauze?

Mrs. Namiki: I am not saying I want one.

Namiki: Why, you can say you want one.

Mrs. Namiki: Because after all we can't afford it, eh?

Namiki: Oh, crazy. Couldn't you keep that back? A word suppressed often makes one that much cleverer. [Mrs. NAMIKI *looks at her husband surprised.*] Good Heavens! When we come here so seldom, I have to meet such a bore.

Mrs. Namiki: Bore? He seems quite nice, doesn't he? But something happened while we were gone? Yes, it was somewhat funny......the way of your greeting......you looked so intimate at first, though.

Namiki: That isn't true. It was the same. [*pause*] He asked me what I was doing at present.

Mrs. Namiki: And what did you say?

Namiki: I told him I was employed at a bookseller's.

Mrs. Namiki: Didn't he ask you what bookseller's?

Namiki: No, he didn't. He's not interested in such things. But he asked me about you.

Mrs. Namiki: What did he ask?

Namiki: Such as from what school you had graduated......and he was also praising you so much that I felt uncomfortable.

Mrs. Namiki: Well, how?

Namiki: Why, many ways. He's a rude fellow. He said he'd loan me money whenever I was in a tight place.

Mrs. Namiki: Oh, my,......but he seems to appreciate our situation, doesn't he?

Namiki : Say, a fellow can't talk about such when he meets an old friend. I told him, " Don't be silly ! "

Mrs. Namiki : Oh, you shouldn't have said such things, when he said that out of kindness. Is that why you refused to dine with them ?

Namiki : Yes. [*pause*] Shall I borrow some money from him and buy a *hitoe-obi* ?

Mrs. Namiki : Could you do that......?

Namiki : Sure. I can do it if I have a mind to......

Mrs. Namiki : You're not serious......

Namiki : Why ? Why can't I do that ?

Mrs. Namiki : I wouldn't want you to do a thing like that, even if we were really hard up.

Namiki [*with a serious look*] : I would do it, if it were for you.

Mrs. Namiki [*deeply moved*] : It's more than enough for me to have you just say so. [*Suddenly changing her tone.*] Darling, will you please not force yourself to do anything against your will ? I'm getting a little scared. [NAMIKI *does not answer*] I can hardly bear the idea that you should feel small before an old friend.

Namiki : I am not saying anything. Only that fellow......

Mrs. Namiki : Yes, I know that. So please give him a flat refusal at such a time......only without hurting his feelings. [*pause*] I'll never say I want anything from now on.

Namiki: But that's different. If we can afford it, why that's all right.

Mrs. Namiki: No. So please keep up such a fine relationship with all your friends that you don't have to humble yourself.

Namiki: You needn't worry about that.

Mrs. Namiki: Sure, it's something to worry about. I......I hadn't realized it before......just that one thing.

Namiki: That one thing......?

Mrs. Namiki: Will you please get a job soon, instead of loafing around all the time, my dear? If we ever get any money, let's save it, and not buy a *hitoe-obi*.

Namiki: Why, this is funny......for you suddenly to say things like that.

Mrs. Namiki [*with tears in her eyes*]: Yes, ...to be sure, there must be a reason. But...... but......you know, you're gradually losing all your good friends.

[*Suddenly she begins to cry, burying her face in her husband's chest.*]

— *Curtain* —

LIVING KOHEIJI

BY SENSABURO SUZUKI

A PLAY IN THREE ACTS

"LIVING KOHEIJI"

A PLAY IN THREE ACTS

By Sensaburo Suzuki

Translated by Noboru Hidaka

Characters : *Koheiji Kobata*, an actor
Takuro Nako, a drummer for a
Japanese orchestra
Ochika, Takuro's wife
Time : *Yedo* Period

ACT I

[*On the* Asakanuma *pond in* Kohoriyama, Oushiu. *At the end of April by the lunar calendar. Turbid water darkly shadowed by overspreading trees. The sky is cloudy as if it is threatening to rain ; but far beyond the mountains there is a bit of blue sky from where the faint sun-beams are streaming down on the surface of the water.*

A small boat in the center ; KOHEIJI *and* TAKURO *are discovered angling from the boat. All is quiet.*]

Takuro : What time will it be now ? [KOHEIJI *does not answer.*] Tut, tut ! Again, it was cut ! [*A splash.*] Look ! It is biting ! What are you dreaming about ?

Koheiji [*as if awakened from a trance*]: Ah, y...e...s.

Takuro : It looks like a big carp ! Oh, no, that is not the way ! [*The fish escapes the hook. A pause.*] How could you make such a foolish pull ? Holy smoke ! You know the line never misses breaking if you make such foolish pulls. [KOHEIJI *does not answer.*] Hey, look at this crucian ! It's as big as a black beam-fish ! [*He takes the fish from the hook and throws the line again into the water with a new bait*] Hei-ho, hei-ho, one more hei-ho, an' pull with all might an' main. [*He sings.*]

E'en hearin' your voice so sweet,
I feel my poor limbs numbed......

Koheiji [*as if whispering*]:

Still more so if I could have you, stronger than death will be......

[TAKURO *stares at* KOHEIJI. *A long pause. Suddenly as if getting impatient.*] Say, what time is it now ?

Takuro : Well, [*pause*] I think it is past four.

Koheiji : The setting sun surely makes one feel lonesome, doesn't it ?

Takuro: Yes. This road of Oushiu is gloomier than any other I know of.

Koheiji [*a pause. Then, as if talking to himself*]: I should like to go back to Yedo quick.

Takuro: Are you so lonesome? [*He laughs.*]

Koheiji [*after a pause*]: It's already more than seventy days since we left Yedo.

Takuro: That's right. [*pause*] And I know that you are not yet used to travel.

[*A long silence.*]

Koheiji: Now, Takuro.

Takuro: What?

Koheiji: I have one favor to beg of you. [TAKURO *looks up.*] I hope you won't be angry.

Takuro: No. But I can't tell how I will feel until I hear your story.

Koheiji: To tell you the truth, it is about Ochika-san.

Takuro: Ochika-san? [*pause*] Let me see, will that be my wife Ochika?

Koheiji [*with uneasiness*]: Yes.

[*A long pause.*]

Takuro [*surlily*]: Anyway, go ahead and tell it what?

Koheiji: Why, yes. For a long time, I have been trying to make a clean breast of it......after we go back to Yedo, I will have no chance to do that, and then......[*Suddenly he stops.*]

[*A long pause. A* hototogisu *heard chirruping in the sky.* KOHEIJI *looks up.*]

Takuro: What's the matter? I am waiting for your story.

Koheiji: Takuro! For a long time, you have been despising me secretly, I suppose.

Takuro: Why do you talk like that?

Koheiji: I am so sorry. Forgive me. [TAKURO *smokes from a Japanese pipe; the ashes fall down on the water only to die away.*] Of course, I don't think I can be excused by only an apology. Please feel for me. [TAKURO *does not answer.*] I am ashamed that I have pretended to be your good friend for these years. Please do forgive me. [TAKURO *still does not answer.*] When people are already chattering about us now, you may well think it is so brazen-faced of me to ask so shamelessly your forgiveness. I know well that you have been angry with me all this time. [TAKURO *sneers at him.*] And yet. I am going to broach this subject......[*pause*] What would you say? [*Faltering.*] a......a......well, couldn't you give up Ochika-san to me?

Takuro: Gracious! You know she is my wife.

Koheiji: That's a poser. [*pause*] Poor as I am, I am still the fag-end of an actor. I don't like to bring up such a ridiculous matter in earnest.

But I ask you this after brooding over it. Please understand me......[*pause*] As you remain silent about it, I am much more pained. If I go on like this any longer, I will go crazy. [*Still* TAKURO *sneers at him.*] I would rather wish to be kicked and put to shame in the green-room before the director and friends, then I would feel easy at heart. It is hard for me to be left as I am for ever. I am sorry. I don't know how to apologize.

Takuro [*after a pause, coldly*]: Of course I am an insignificant drummer for the show, but I have lived in the theatre ever since I was sixteen. Do you think I would make such a fuss over my wife's fliration? [KOHEIJI *does not answer.*] Especially when it is within her means to keep company with actors? Is there anything for me to do but to pretend not to know?

Koheiji: What? to keep company with actors, you say that?

Takuro: Exactly.

Koheiji: Oh, yes, I am an actor, but I tell you, I have never been hired by the wife of a friend. (Note: Actors were often hired by rich women as male-geishas or male-prostitutes.)

Takuro: What!

Koheiji: Ochika and I have been in love for more than four years, ever since she was widowed by the death of Hanroku Sugiyama. Maybe fate was against me, or I wasn't good enough; before I knew it, you and Ochika-san were married.

Takuro: Surely, I had the first chance, and I got her for my wife.

Koheiji: What I have done since then must be wrong. Of course I should be blamed for it. But it is not that I fooled her for the amusement of the hour nor was I fooled by her. She was the one to whom I lost my heart from the first, and whom I made my true love.

Takuro: I don't know about things of the past. Well, anyhow there is no mistaking that she is a respectable married woman now. So it is Koheiji Kobata, the actor, whom she hired, isn't it?

Koheiji: Still do you say so? [*pause*] When I have suffered in this bitter love for these years, believing that you considered me your friend......I have a sin on my conscience if you talk like that. Though I have come down to an actor's life, I am a man! Listen, I am not such a mean fellow as you think! [TAKURO *laughs.*] I have never done anything with a woman whom I didn't love. I murmer complaints and do wrongs because I love her so much. If it were just for a whim, how would I make an advance to a mere drummer's wife?

Takuro: What the hell......?

Koheiji: Give me leave to say that I have never fallen in love without sincerity.

Takuro [*laughing*]: After you have stolen your friend's wife, what a show you make in the boat! Well, is that some characterization of a great actor of old, or what? Cut the stuff, please! [KOHEIJI *is silent.*] The audacity of evil-doers, indeed!

Koheiji: Perhaps I talked too much, please forgive me. There must be something wrong with me. Pray forgive me everything, and give her up to me. Let me marry her, I beg of you, yes, I entreat you. I just can't forget her. [TAKURO *does not answer.*] If it were a love I could forget, I wouldn't ask you for such an unusual favor. Please forget and forgive everything, I beg you.

Takuro [*after a pause*]: You say that after you have talked with Ochika? Tut! tut! I shouldn't have listened to such a thing.

Koheiji: That isn't so. You should have known what kind of woman she is. She is a weak, tender-hearted creature. Finding herself between two fires, she is living in fear and trembling all year around, afraid something might happen at any moment and praying to God that the affair between us should be smoothed over. That's the kind of woman she is. That's why I ask your favor. She is weak, and she isn't a

woman who could desert you and come to me.
Neither do I like to steal a march upon you and
have her play such a mean trick.   There is no
other means for us to get married except by
your help.   You and I have been good friends for
ages.   I take advantage of our friendship to beg
of you such a delicate favor.   It rests with you
whether she as well as I will be saved from the
hell......

Takuro: Instead of you, I should be fallen
into the hell, is that what you mean?   That is
not fair!   I won't.   By God I won't.

[*Long pause.*]

Koheiji: Why not?

Takuro: Well, I will tell you once for all,
so don't forget; she is my wife!   [KOHEIJI *does not
answer.*]   Don't think we are married without love!
You get me?   [KOHEIJI *is still silent.*]   In fact, you
are a light-hearted man!   Maybe you are taking
the matter too simply.   Since she has another
fellow she loves, and since she is such an evil-
minded wife and a bitch who disgraces her husband,
why should I not drive her out?   That is what you
are thinking, eh?   [KOHEIJI *does not answer.*]   Bah!
Too bad, things don't go so well.   If I had my
way, I would have made myself master of the
Empire.   A woman who is loved by a man, is
loved by others, too.   I tell you, it is not that I

don't love Ochika. Hum. How inconsiderate of you not to realize it! If you do, what a cool fish you are! [KOHEIJI *is silent.*] It seems to me that it is about time that even Ochika should have her eyes opened. In fact, her dream was too long. [*Sneering.*] I have always been sorry for you. Though you are a playmate to please her whims now, someday I am quite sure she is going to ditch you. I have noticed that you used to avoid any good contract if it was a local performance for which you had to leave Yedo, and I have secretly pitied you. Perhaps you have been the loser in many ways. You may have missed even the chance of success for all I know. I thought that these resignations were all for my wife's sake, and I have wished to tell you sooner or later that I was sorry for you. [KOHEIJI *turns pale with indignation.*] I love Ochika as well as you do; there are many ways to love a woman. You may think I should treat her more considerately if I love her. But I have my own way of doing things. Well, I will make it clear to you. No matter how harshly I may treat her, I do love her, too. [KOHEIJI *is still quiet.*] If you want to take her from me, you are an actor, try to make her desert me! Mind you, don't hesitate but go ahead and let her run to you! Various arts of love-making! Guiles to win girls in the love-scene! Do your very best with all these! Wasn't a *jeune premier* your part in character?

Koheiji: Certainly I am not without the knowledge of the guiles and tricks of love, but if one is truly in love, one can't play double. I am in dead earnest. So I have been tortured with the pain of love. And like a fool I begged you for a favor.

Takuro: Hum. That's too bad, I should say. Why, a woman's heart depends on herself. For instance, I can't tell it either. There is no help for it. Well, let's fight it out! You may well strive to the utmost to take Ochika away from me! [*pause*] Now, let's drop this subject.

Koheiji: You won't listen to me, then? [TAKURO *does not answer.*] Very well, then, [*After a pause.*] I won't ask you any more. [TAKURO *still silent.*] Since she is the first woman with whom I have ever fallen so madly in love, I surely will fight to the finish. [*pause*] By Jove, I will make her my wife! [TAKURO *does not say anything. As if whispering.*] You said she was just after an actor, eh? [*pause*] If you don't take me seriously, it can't be helped now. I will show you what true love can do. [TAKURO *sneers at him.*] You told me, a woman's heart depends on herself, eh? Don't ever forget that!

Takuro: It is my nature to think highly of

myself......[*Laughing*.] Ochika and I are in every respect turtle-doves.

Koheiji [*ghastly*]: But you know there are some separate turtle-doves!

Takuro [*after a long pause*]: " Wives of other people an' flowers of the bamboo, Don't take ever fancy to them! Only disappointed you will be," so it is sung in the ballad of Yahata. Koheiji, I feel so wretched! I will tell you as a friend, don't go too deep and don't be carried off by the waves. Don't make yourself turn into an ear-shell by being swallowed into the bottom of the sea. You should know when to stop.

Koheiji: None of your sauce! Now, Ochika is not my friend's wife any more; she is but a woman under the sun. You shall see what a power my love has.

Takuro: But remember the supernatural powers the husband gets. Very often a sudden change of the scene is made at the last moment. Don't trip!

Koheiji: Well, dote on your wife as much as possible! Cantharides in the morning tea! A *chin* venom in the night-cup! Take care that she doesn't poison you!

Takuro: What do you say? [*Changing his color*.] What in the world do you mean by that?

Koheiji: Now I don't care for disgrace or

scandal. If only I had my life to live with her! Depend on it I will take her from you!

Takuro: Hum. What would you do if......
you lost that precious life of yours?

Koheiji: Of course, I do stake my life on it. [*Laughs.*] I am going to put all my strength in it.

Takuro: That's fine! Now take this!

Koheiji: What?

[TAKURO *hits* KOHEIJI's *forehead hard with a shipplank.* KOHEIJI *falls down with a scream.*]

Takuro: I will be the one to remain in this world! It is time for you to give up her! [*He hits* KOHEIJI *again. Twilight closes.* KOHEIJI *falls into the pond. Wind blows a little. Suddenly frightened,* TAKURO *begins to row the boat. From the bow creeps up bloody* KOHEIJI, *wound round in sea-weeds.*] God d—n you! [*Gives* KOHEIJI *a drubbing, and again thrusts him in the pond. As the water splash dies away, a* hototogisu *is heard chirruping in the distance for a while.* TAKURO *suddenly cries, looking around the dark water.*] Oh! He is still alive! [*Unconsciously he lets go the oar, and the boat turns round.*] By Heavens, you shall not escape me! [*He rows again.*]

— Curtain —

ACT II

[*About ten days later,* TAKURO'S *two-storied house near the River* Sumida, Yedo. *Evening. The river is heard flowing. Green hare's-foot ferns are hanging from the eaves. The high walls surrounding the house next door are far at the back. The big pine-tree in the chevaux-de-frise hangs over this small house.*

OCHIKA *is combing her hair at the mirror.* KOHEIJI *comes in panting hard,—with a death-like face and fresh wounds. He peeps inside from the gate. He is walking around outside for a while.*

It rains a little harder. The stage darkens a bit.]

Koheiji [*in a low voice*]: Ochika-san ! [OCHIKA *strains her ears.*] Ochika-san !

Ochika: Yes. Who is it ?

Koheiji: It's me !

Ochika: Who ? [*Stands up to see* KOHEIJI, *but cannot recognize him well.*] Will you please open there ?

Koheiji [*in a low voice*]: It's me. It's Koheiji.

Ochika: Koheiji-san ? Oh, my......

Koheiji: Can you spare me a little while ? Just come out over here.

[OCHIKA *opens the door.*]

Ochika: Why, what happened? What is this? For Heaven's sake, how you look!

Koheiji: I have struggled to reach here...... I have not even gone home yet.

Ochika: Takuro is not with you?

Koheiji: No, I am alone.

Ochika: Really what happened? Oh dear, you are so badly wounded! Did you have anything go wrong on the road? [KOHEIJI *does not answer*.] Anyhow, come inside. There is nobody. I have been so much worried.

Koheiji: Worried......? About Takuro? or about me?

[OCHIKA *does not answer*.]

Ochika: Why, anyway you should come in first and change those clothes of yours. How pale you look! and so wounded, too......[KOHEIJI *tries to smile faintly*.] My darling, your face is just like a dead man's. [*pause*] What on earth happened on the road? Please tell me.

Koheiji: Yes! [*Impatiently*.] Ochika-san! I've wanted to see you so much.

[*Takes her hands*.]

Ochika [*slightly confused*]: I, too......

Koheiji: Ochika-san, Takuro that you are waiting for will never come back now.

Ochika: Never come back?......What do you mean?

Koheiji: He is dead. [OCHIKA *is silent.*]
Takuro was killed.

Ochika: Is that true? By whom? and how?

Koheiji: He was killed by me......by this
Koheiji Kobata. [OCHIKA *keeps silence.*] What
will you do, my dear? [*Takes her hands again.*]
I tell you I have killed him.

Ochika: Could it be possible that such......
such a thing happened?

Koheiji: Do you think it isn't possible.

Ochika: But how you......?

Koheiji: Do you think I can't do that?
[OCHIKA *does not answer.*] I've done it. I certainly
killed Takuro. He isn't in this world any more.

Ochika: Ah! [*After a pause.*] Aren't you
crazy?

Koheiji: I couldn't let him have you longer.
[*pause*] I killed him at Kohoriyama. I took him
out on the Asakanuma pond, and I stabbed him
to death in the boat. [OCHIKA *is silent.*] I threw
his body in the pond. Do you hear, in the pond.
[OCHIKA *staggers in amazement.*] I left the place
on the instant. Look, this wound on my forehead
is also what I got at that time. It's the one that
Takuro......Takuro inflicted on me. [*pause*] I was
beaten and beaten, and knocked down. [*pause*]
That confounded fellow! [*Still* OCHIKA *keeps
silence.*] Well, that's that. But the trouble is

that the police seem to have learned about this already.

Ochika: Ah! What shall I do?

Koheiji: You and I have been in this relation for a long time, and everybody knows about us now. So they will soon find out that you were the cause of the fight. [OCHIKA *weeps.*] Should I be arrested tonight, I will state that I have conspired together with you to kill him. I wish you would understand it so, too. [*pause*] You won't mind, eh?

Ochika: How can it......?

Koheiji: You don't mean to say that it can't be done, I hope? Ochika, I know you can't be such a faithless woman.

Ochika: But......

Koheiji: Even if I don't talk about it, people will still gossip freely about us so. [*pause*] My dear, you haven't come to hate me? [OCHIKA *does not answer.*] Or do you look upon me as your husband's slayer? [OCHIKA *still does not answer.*] Kill me if you hate me. I don't hold my life dear. I have lived on only for you. Or you may as well hand me over to the police. I won't do anything. [OCHIKA *is stubbornly silent.*] At any rate I am going to tell them in the first place that I have done it in collusion with you.

Ochika: My dear......

Koheiji: Ochika-san, I don't want to die yet. I want to live. I should like to have a warm dream once more with you. Please take pity on me! Please sympathize with me!

Ochika: Koheiji-san. [*Weeps.*] Forgive me.

Koheiji: Ochika-san! Won't you run away with me to Yedo? [OCHIKA *does not answer.*] If I get caught in the meantime, I won't go to the prison-gate or die on the cross alone, as people know about us and wouldn't doubt what I say. By God, I will take you with me on the road to death. [OCHIKA *keeps silent.*] But I want to live. Please run away with me to Kamigata at once. [OCHIKA *still weeps.*] Since you had two men, you couldn't expect things to come round in the end. You must have known that some day there would be a desperate struggle between us to take you or to give you up, didn't you? Since we have come to this, there is little to think about now. To be executed together on the charge of killing Takuro, or to leave this place before we attract notice! We have to take one of the two courses, haven't we?

Ochika: Yes.

Koheiji: It was only because I wanted to win you that I killed my rival Takuro. Please run away with me! Say you will run away with me!

Ochika: All right.

Koheiji: Won't you link your destiny with mine and think of ours as a fatal connection? [*Weeps.*]   Please take pity on me.

Ochika [*weeping*]:   I know.   I understand well how you feel.   Let's live as much as we can, and let's die when the time comes.

Koheiji: Oh, then, you will go with me? [OCHIKA *nods.*]   The rain has stopped, and the sun is setting.   Please pack up your things as quickly as possible.   Let's start at once.   You can make small preparations on the way.

Ochika: Well, I will.   Please wait for me a minute.   I know there is some money in a small bureau upstairs.......I will take that.

Koheiji [*nods*]:   But please hurry.

Ochika: All right, dear.   Wait for me, I will be down in a jiffy.

[OCHIKA *enters the room, and goes upstairs. After a while,* TAKURO *comes along in a traveling outfit.* KOHEIJI *squats down on the floor furtively.*]

Takuro [*at the entrance*]:   Ochika!   Ochika! [*There is no answer.*]   Hallo, Ochika!   Tut! tut!   [*He takes off his sandals.*]   Well, well, I am so tired.   [*Looks at* KOHEIJI.]   Who are you? Who is crouching there?   [KOHEIJI *stands up in silence.*]   Who are you?   [*Screams.*]   You......

are......Koheiji ?

Koheiji [*gloomily*] : Yes !

Takuro : Damnation ! You still can't die, eh ?

Koheiji : No. [TAKURO *draws his sword. Despairingly.*] Will you do that ? [*pause*] Will you kill me again ? [TAKURO *does not answer.*] Kill me if you like ! I won't lift my finger against you. Staggering along all the way, stambling over even small stones and grass-roots, I could barely reach here. Look at these hands like a dead man's, and look at this face......... [TAKURO *groans with agony.*] I am as good as dead. Do whatever you like with me ! Kill me if you want ! [TAKURO *is silent.*] You won't kill me ? [TAKURO *does not answer.*] My body may die, but my spirit won't ! Now, try and see ! [TAKURO *keeps silence. Very gloomily.*] Kill me quick !

Takuro [*almost screaming*] : Forgive me ! [KOHEIJI *does not answer.*] I can't kill you. Ah ! I am so afraid ! [KOHEIJI *keeps silence.*] I will give O......Ochika to you. Take her away ! I can't stand this any longer. I......I can't !

Koheiji : Do you mean it ?

Takuro : How can I tell a lie ? I mean it. I mean it ! [*Trembling all over.*] I am scared ! I lost the game. Your face which I saw on the

water ! I had thought it was only a phantom......
That you would ever come back here......, that
you would ever come back to life......! Oh!
save my soul! Forgive me! Take Ochika away
with you!

[OCHIKA *comes downstairs.*]

Ochika: Oh dear! Aren't you Takuro-dono?
So you are still alive, dear?

Takuro: Ochika !

Ochika: Koheiji-san, so you made up such a
story......that you killed Takuro? Great Heavens,
what a terrible lie you told!

Koheiji: Ochika-san. Please be my wife.

Ochika: Dear me......how......?

Koheiji: Takuro says so, too. Please come
along with me.

Ochika: So you say, but......

Takuro [*avoiding her eyes*]: Go! go! please
be gone! I am sick and tired of everything
now.

Ochika: Gracious! I can't understand this!

Takuro [*muttering*]: I am tired of it. I am
afraid. I am sick of it now.

Koheiji: Let's go......let's go as an honest
couple in the sight of Heaven!

Ochika [*pause*]: Takuro-dono, do you also
tell me to go? [TAKURO *does not answer.*] Pray!
do you really mean to say so?

Koheiji: Ochika-san!

Ochika: Takuro-dono, do you want to part from me?

Takuro [*looks at* OCHIKA]: Ochika!

Koheiji: It is a promise! Ochika-san. [*Takes her hands.*] Now, let's go quick!

[TAKURO *ventures to give* KOHEIJI *a cut with his sword. With a shriek* KOHEIJI *grapples with* TAKURO. OCHIKA *grasps* KOHEIJI'S *foot. He falls down.* TAKURO *bestrides on* KOHEIJI *and stabs him.*]

Ochika: That's it. Well done! You dirty liar! [TAKURO *takes off his sword by putting his foot on* KOHEIJI'S *body.*] On his throat! One more stab on his throat!

Takuro: It's enough. It's enough, now! To be sure, he must be dead this time. Ah!

Ochika: Thank Heaven! Ah! how scared I was! Look how I am trembling......it was a narrow escape......

Takuro: At last he is dead. [*A long pause. Suddenly he begins to cry like a child.*] Ah! at last I've killed......killed my old friend.

[*She gazes at him a minute; then she suddenly hugs him passionately.*]

— *Curtain* —

ACT III

[*All is dark, and nothing is seen. The roar of the sea is heard. At the center of the stage*, TAKURO *and* OCHIKA *are discovered resting on something. They are in traveling outfits.*]

Takuro [*after a long silence*]: Well! Let's be going.

Ochika: Please let me rest some more. It seems I can't walk a step farther.

Takuro: Try to stand up. You shouldn't be so done in yet.

Ochika: Oh! don't be so cruel, dear! I tell you I am tired out.......

Takuro: I am tired, too. But we have to pass through the next post-town by morning.

Ochika: I can't go so far.

Takuro: Do you think we can stay here like this because you're tired? [OCHIKA *does not answer.*] Come on! Try to stand up!

Ochika [*tries to stand up, but gives up at once*]: It's no use.

Takuro: That can't be. · I have walked as much as you did. Keep up your spirits! brace yourself! Well, try to stand up!

Ochika: I cannot. [TAKURO *is silent.*] I am completely done.

Takuro: Well, what are you going to do,

then ?

Ochika: I should like to rest here.

Takuro: It will be morning soon.

Ochika: I don't mind if it is morning.

Takuro: Don't forget that the policemen are after us.

Ochika: Oh! indeed......[*pause*] Howm any days already have we walked in this fear! And I wonder how many days more, how many years more we shall have to walk in fear and trembling?

Takuro: It will be ended soon.

Ochika: To be sure, soon we will be dead. Oh! God! I'm sick!

Takuro: No, I said it will be ended soon. Four or five days more, and then we can have plenty of time for rest. If we go as far as Nako, we are safe.

Ochika: I am well content with this spot. [*pause*] Oh, what a dark night it is! There isn't a star. Listen, we can hear the sea, can't we? [*pause*] Autumn is close at hand now. [*pause*] Dear, it is almost three months since the thing happened, isn't it?

Takuro: Please don't talk about that, will you? [*After a pause.*] Didn't you notice a man standing in the shadow of a paper-lamp in front of the inn last night?

Ochika: No, I didn't. I......

Takuro: He was the very image of Koheiji. [*pause*] Say, Koheiji is not dead. [*pause*] I didn't tell you for fear that you would be frightened, but I heard that he had come to life again......

Ochika: What silly talk !

Takuro: Yes, it is true. He has a wonderful life. I certainly killed him once at the Asakanuma pond, and you know what happened then......living again, he came to Yedo.

Ochika: But you did' run him through with your sword that time, didn't you ?

Takuro: Yes, I ran him through. And we fled from the house.

Ochika: Ever since then we have been traveling thus......for three months......No wonder I am tired.

Takuro: I was told that Koheiji had got his breath after he had received proper treatment. He must be living somewhere ! [*pause*] He is a fellow who would never die however many times you might kill him. He is a ghost.

Ochika: Could such a strange story be possible ? Who told you such things ? Isn't it absurd ?

Takuro: Sometime ago when we were hiding at a temple, I once went down town. I met Yashichi of Yamamura-za, and he told me all this. I have kept it to myself until now, but......it is true. [OCHIKA *does not speak.*] And I saw Koheiji myself. [*pause*] That we left the inn in such a hurry was not because of the policemen, but because I saw Koheiji. That's why we stole a march on him at midnight. There was a fellow looking at us stealthily under the paper-lamp, and it must have been Koheiji.

Ochika : That must be some mistake. There's no explaining how he could come this far, is there ? [*pause*] How did he look, though? that man ?

Takuro : I couldn't see anything but his face, but it was as pale as paper, and he looked thin. I am quite sure that he is following us. He must have been traveling after us for a long time. What a vindictive beast !

Ochika : I can hardly believe it.

Takuro : Yes, it is true. He is waiting for the chance to catch us napping. He is like a snake. He is trying to wreak his vengeance on us. [*pause*] That's why I am hurrying. [OCHIKA *is silent.*] I think he is determined to get you at any risk. Oh ! what a person !

Ochika : But even he must have given up hope. There is something wrong with your eyes, my dear.

Takuro : No. I certainly saw him. [*pause*] Now, let's go quick. Really we can't be dawdling like this. Let's go so far Koheiji can't reach us.

Ochika : But if he were alive ?......Could such a thing be possible in this world ?

Takuro : Possible or impossible, we have to move on anyhow. We have no time to lose, have we ?

Ochika : But, it's no use for me. I am so tired I can't walk any more.

Takuro : Aren't you afraid of Koheiji ?

Ochika : If he were alive, we could escape the punishment, though. As it means that we haven't committed murder, our crime will be far lighter.

Takuro : But Koheiji won't look at it that way. I am all the more afraid because he is alive.

Ochika : You may as well kill him again ......kill him over and over again.

Takuro : Ah ! [*pause*] This may be your true character, then. But I can't do such a thing any more. No, never !

Ochika : Then we shall be killed instead.

Takuro : That's why, am I not telling you to set out quick ?

Ochika : But......would Koheiji kill me too ? that man......? [TAKURO *does not answer.*] Say, dear, what do you think ?

Takuro : I don't know. I......I have never thought of that.

Ochika : I bet you that things will turn out

well.

Takuro: What a dreadful woman you are! Wasn't it you who made me kill Koheiji that time? When I remember that you helped me kill him, I feel mean and wretched.

Ochika: Weren't you going to kill him at the Asakanuma, though? And even before I did anything, you were going to kill him alone, isn't that so?

Takuro: Yes. But if it were not for you, I would never have made him suffer such a horrible experience.

Ochika: You say I am responsible for everything, eh?

Takuro: Forgive me. I didn't mean that ......I was surely to blame...... [*pause*] But I do feel as if you would marry him with perfect indifference if Koheiji succeeded in killing me. I can't endure......that idea.

Ochika: Really, you have become suspicious lately. The other day, you suspected me of having something to do with a man in the next room at the inn......

Takuro: Every man looks like Koheiji to me. [*pause*] Well, never mind. Let's be going now. [*pause*] Hey!

Ochika: Won't you squeeze me tight for once, darling? squeeze me tight...... [TAKURO *does not answer.*] Hold me tight and cheer me up. As it is, I feel so disheartened I can't stand up. If I don't burn up my emotion, my body and legs won't work. [*pause*] Won't you hug me, dear?

Takuro [*startled as he is about to hug her*]: Ah!

Ochika: What's the matter? to scream like that......?

Takuro: Oh! [*After a while.*] Just......just now didn't you see somebody was standing between you and me?

Ochika: How silly! It's only your fancy. Please keep up your spirits, dear. [TAKURO *stretches his hands, but draws them back at once. After a pause.*] Very well, then, I shall be sitting thus for ever. For I am neither a bit afraid of the policemen nor of Koheiji now.

Takuro [*with a deep sigh*]: When you were such a timid, tender-hearted creature before, how could you talk like that?

Ochika: But I am so tired, my body and legs are all limp. [*Wind blowing.*] Oh! I am chilly! [*pause*] A cold wind blows from the sea-shore, doesn't it?

Takuro: Maybe it is blowing from Hades.

Ochika: I am so cold! Won't you hug me tight, dear?

Takuro: No......no, I won't. I can't help thinking that there is somebody between you and me. I feel I hug the strange fellow instead of you...... [*pause*] somebody like Koheiji. [OCHIKA *laughs*.] Try to touch me with your hand, will you? Somehow I can't stop trembling.

Ochika: It's dark. It's pitch-dark! [*Holding out her hand, she reaches for him.*] Look here! It's all right. There is nobody.

Takuro: Oh! what cold hands! Are these your hands?

Ochika [*silent for a while*]: You have warm hands, dear. [*Leans over him.* TAKURO *puts her back in a hurry in silence.*] What's the matter?

Takuro: No. I am scared. [*Starting.*] I will go alone. I......I am going alone after all.

Ochika: Won't you take me?

Takuro: You go back to Yedo! [*As he is about to go.*] Oh, I have to go alone.

Ochika [*rising*]: Are you going away, and leave me in such a place? How could you do such an unfaithful thing?

Takuro: I can't help it. [*Begins to walk.*] I am going. [*pause*] I go alone. It's a long journey.

Ochika: Pray take me with you, dear. I beg you, don't desert me......

Takuro: Is that until you get a better companion ?

Ochika: Why do you say such a thing ?
[*pause*]   Nowadays you often say such queer
things.   [T<small>AKURO</small> *walks away in silence towards the*
o.p. (*opposite-prompter side*) *She follows him.*]
Wait for me !   please wait for me !   Will you
please walk more slowly ? so that I may follow
you...... ?

Takuro: I am hurrying.   I am hurrying.
[O<small>CHIKA</small> *runs inside after him.*]

[*Nobody is on the stage now.*

*From the dark, front, interior, where they have
been resting, comes around a traveler that looks like*
K<small>OHEIJI</small>. *And he plods his lonely way after the
couple.   He disappears in the darkness.*

A long pause.

Darkness.

The roar of the sea......]

— *Curtain* —

THE SAVIOR OF THE MOMENT

BY KWAN KIKUCHI

A DRAMA IN ONE ACT

"THE SAVIOR OF THE MOMENT"

A DRAMA IN ONE ACT

By Kwan Kikuchi

Translated by Noboru Hidaka

Characters : *Eisaku Sagara*, thirty years old,
an impecunious writer
Nuiko, his wife, 24 or 25 years
old
Mrs. Yoshiko Sugimoto, Nuiko's
cousin and about her age

Time : Present
Place : Suburb of Tokyo
Scene : *Eisaku Sagara's* home
[*A three-room cottage with a forest in fresh verdure at the back. A two-mat room for the entrance, and the next is the six-mat room. The entrance cannot be seen by the audience. Against the interior wall of the six-mat room stands a large book case ; about half of the books are in foreign languages. Near the veranda is a desk made of red*

sandalwood, the kind highly prized by writers in Japan.

EISAKU SAGARA, *the master of the house, is lying with his head on a cushion folded fourfold. The four-and-a-half-mat room is the wife's living room. A triple chest of drawers stands against the interior wall. At the right of the drawers is a clothes-rack on which hangs two or three* kimonos *and a faded summer overcoat.*

NUIKO *is unsewing her winter clothes. Now and then she looks towards the next room where* EISAKU *is lying. He has been sleeping for a long time.*]

Nuiko [*as if talking to herself, but in fact to let her husband hear it*]: Today is the 28th, and tomorrow the 29th......there are only four days left, aren't there? [*She is waiting for her husband to answer.*] I wonder when I shall have no more worries about the monthly bills? The house-rent is in arrears for four months, and we can't pay the rent this month, either. I don't know what to do. [*The husband does not say anything.*] If we don't pay the rice-dealer ten or fifteen *yen* by some means or other at the end of this month, he won't bring us any more rice. Really he is such a nice and kind man. We are the ones to be blamed. [*Her voice gets louder.* EISAKU *turns on his side.*] Say, dear! [EISAKU *does not answer.*]

Say, are you awake? [*Still no answer.*] Are you awake, dear? say, aren't you awake?...... [*Getting impatient, she opens the sliding door violently.*]

Eisaku: Fool! [*Shouts in a wild voice.*]

Nuiko: For Heaven's sake, please don't yell so loud! You startle me!

Eisaku: But didn't I tell you never to open this door until I am through with my novel? [*Still lying on his back, he yells at her.*]

Nuiko: But haven't you slept all morning, though you said you were going to write?

Eisaku: I can't help that. When the ideas aren't matured, it's impossible to write even a line no matter now hard one may try.

Nuiko: You say you were waiting for your ideas to mature, but you were snoring loudly just a moment ago, weren't you? Indeed, I am disgusted with all this.

Eisaku: If you are, have your own way and be d—ned!

Nuiko: Certainly I will! By the way, where were you last night?

Eisaku: It's none of your business!

Nuiko: No, maybe not, but if I let you do as you like, I don't know what will become of me. For instance, last night, I am quite sure you went to the Café Printemps after you got the money for your story from the newspaper.

Eisaku: Don't harbour such a nasty suspicion.

Nuiko: Whenever I point out a fault, you always make it my nasty suspicion.

Eisaku: Isn't that right, though? I think it is.

Nuiko: Well......would you call that a nasty suspicion? Please tell me, then, where you got that five-*yen* bill in your sleeve pocket?

Eisaku [*half rising*]: What! Did you search even my sleeve pocket?

Nuiko: Was I wrong to do that?

Eisaku: Certainly you were! Even if you are my wife, you have no right to search my pockets.

Nuiko: But the moment you get any money, you go out to have a good time. It is too much for me. You seek pleasures outside while you put all the trouble upon me at home. Really, this is unbearable. You are after good times as long as your money lasts, and when it's gone you come home for rest. Then where do I come in?

Eisaku: Well, I don't get much of a thrill out of looking at you.

Nuiko: I suppose not. You would get far more of a thrill if you went to the Café Printemps and talked with the waitress you like, wouldn't you?

Eisaku: Hum!

Nuiko: Why "Hum!" Where were you the other night? You told me you were late because you played cards at Mr. Kawase's, but I think it must be a lie.

Eisaku: *Nonsense*!

Nuiko: What's "*Nonsense*"? Do you think I am so dumb as not to know that you are paying attention to some other girl?

Eisaku: Some other girl! If I had one, I would be much happier.

Nuiko: Well, if you don't have any, why don't you come home until late every night?

Eisaku: That's my business.

Nuiko: What business!

Eisaku: Oh! dear me, I am so disgusted. Whenever I am fretful, and have a hard time to write, you always start grumbling about something or other only to irritate me more. Ah Gosh, I wish I could get out somewhere.

Nuiko: Well, I will get out somewhere for you instead. I know you are tired of me anyhow. We've married without love. I will go at once. How much easier it will be to live as a business woman!

Eisaku: What a bore! Oh, how my head throbs!

Nuiko: Yes, I expect so. It must be painful for you to listen to me, as you are tired of me.

But look here, you came home at two o'clock
this morning. And you put all the blame on me
if you can't write. How vexing!

Eisaku: Hey, shut up. I won't talk to you
any more! Now I tell you, don't dare open this!
[*Eisaku shuts the door with a bang.*]

Nuiko: Sure I will open it! [*She opens it
violently. Eisaku turns somewhat pale with anger.*]

Eisaku: Well, try to open it again! I'll beat
you next time. [*He shuts it again.*]

Nuiko: I will open it as often as you shut
it. [*She opens it again roughly. Furious with
anger, Eisaku jumps in the four-and-a-half-mat
room and slaps her face.*] Ouch! [*She cries.*]

Eisaku: Now try to open it. [*He shuts the
door again.*]

Nuiko: Certainly! I will open it even if I
die! [*She jumps at the door, and it falls. Eisaku
slaps her face three or four times. She breaks down
and bursts into tears.*]

Eisaku: Serve you right! [*He shuts the
sliding door, and lies down by the desk again. Nuiko
cries for some time. Then she stands up, opens the
drawers, picks up two or three kimonos and wraps
them in a furoshiki. She goes to the mirror stand,
retouches her face, and then tries to steal away so
that her husband will not notice her. Through the
sliding door.*] Say, are you going out?

Nuiko: Anything wrong with that?

Eisaku: Oh, nothing.

Nuiko: Well then, you mind your own business.

Eisaku: Hm! That may be so. But where are you going?

Nuiko: No other place to go but......to my elder sister's.

Eisaku: Is that so?

Nuiko: Yes, that is so.

Eisaku: Do you know what she thinks of us?

Nuiko: Yes, I do. She always says that I should get a divorce from you.

Eisaku: Very well. If you go to her place, it may mean an end to our relationship.

Nuiko: Yes, I know that much.

Eisaku: All right, then. I just warned you for fear you were taking your step unmindful of the consequences.

Nuiko: You needn't worry.

Eisaku: Very well, then, go!

Nuiko: Sure I am going! [*As if remembering something as she is about to go.*] Oh, I almost forgot that the gas fire was on.

[*She goes in the kitchen, when a woman's voice is heard at the entrance.*]

XX: Good day! May I come in? [Eisaku

waits for NUIKO *to come out, but she does not come out.*] Good day! May I come in?

[NUIKO *does not come out yet. Peeping into the kitchen for a moment and failing to find her there,* EISAKU *goes out to the entrance.*]

Eisaku: Who are you, may I ask?

X X: Is this Mr. Eisaku Sagara's......the one who writes novels?

Eisaku: Yes, it is.

X X: Is Nuiko-san in? I am her cousin, Yoshiko Sugimoto.

Eisaku: Oh, I see. Then you live in Yokohama?

Yoshiko: Yes.

Eisaku: Well, wait a minute, please. [EISAKU *returns to the four-and-a-half-mat room, and yells as he peeps into the kitchen.*] I say! Here's a guest! [NUIKO *comes out in a flurry.*]

Nuiko: Who......?

Eisaku: Yoshiko-san from Yokohama.

Nuiko [*with a perplexed and surprised look*]: Oh my! Yoshiko-san! [*She conceals the* furoshiki *quickly in the closet, and goes to the entrance.*] Hello! How do you do?

Yoshiko: How do you do?

Nuiko: I am so glad that you have come. Really this is a surprise!

Yoshiko: It's a long time since we met last,

isn't it ? It must be almost three years.

Nuiko : Well, please come in.

Yoshiko : Thank you. [*She comes in with a* furoshiki *much like the one* NUIKO *made.*]

Nuiko : Indeed, we haven't seen each other for a long time. I hope you are well. Will you excuse me for my not calling on you for all this while ?

Yoshiko : Why, yes. Please excuse me for not calling on you, too. I am glad to see that you are getting along all right.

Eisaku [*he is in a fidget for a while, but at last he greets her*]: I am Sagara. Very pleased to meet you.

Yoshiko : So am I glad to meet you. I have heard about you for a long time.

Nuiko : I have been so much wishing you would visit us for once.

Yoshiko : I came to Tokyo last January with my husband, but you know it's quite a way to come here from Ginza.

Nuiko : Yes, indeed. It takes longer to come here from Ginza than from Yokohama to Tokyo, doesn't it ?

Yoshiko : Yes, it does.

Nuiko : By the way, thank you for the letter you sent me at the time of the great earthquake. Are the temporary buildings all up in Yokohama now ?

Yoshiko :   They are not making so much progress as in Tokyo.

Eisaku :   I heard your house escaped the fire, but I guess the walls fell down ?

Yoshiko :   Yes, a great many walls fell.

Nuiko :   Is your husband still working in the foreign concern ?

Yoshiko [*with somewhat plaintive expression for a second*] :   Yes.

Nuiko :   He didn't come with you today ?

Yoshiko :   No.

Nuiko :   Are you alone ?

Yoshiko :   Yes.

Nuiko :   Have you come on business to Tokyo ?

Yoshiko :   I have left home.

Nuiko :   You've left home ?

Yoshiko :   Yes, I won't go home for good.

Nuiko :   Why, dear !   What happened ?

Eisaku :   Did you quarrel with your husband ?

Yoshiko :   Yes, that's it.

Nuiko :   Is that true ? .

Yoshiko :   Yes, that's true.

Nuiko :   But I was told your husband was a very kind man.

Yoshiko :   Why, yes, he is, but......

Nuiko :   Why did you quarrel, then ?

Yoshiko :   Well, you see, he does not understand me in the least.

Nuiko : Is that so ?

Eisaku : What was the direct cause of the quarrel ?

Yoshiko [*looking down bashfully*] : I am so ashamed......

Eisaku : I suppose you are. [*He laughs loudly.*]

Nuiko : But are you sure that you aren't going home ?

Yoshiko : Yes, I won't go home.

Nuiko : What are you going to do, then ?

Yoshiko : Won't there be some job for me in Tokyo ?

[NUIKO *does not answer.*]

Eisaku [*to* NUIKO] : You seem to have something in mind. You often say you would like to be a business woman yourself, don't you ?

Nuiko [*grinning*] : I have no such idea in mind.

Yoshiko : I will do anything. I don't mind if it is a house-maid's job.

Nuiko : There are many ads in the papers, but it is hard to get a good place when you actually need it.

Yoshiko : Don't you know of something such as an assistantship to a magazine editor ? I thought I might get such a position if I came over here.

Eisaku [*forcing a smile*]:   There are so many applicants for such openings, you know.

Nuiko: We often talk about business women, but it is very hard to find a good place when you are in want of it.

Yoshiko: But I think we shall find it if we look for it with much patience.   And if I get any job, I will stick to it, and try to have a new life.

Nuiko: Why, yes!   If you do anything intently......[*She drops the conversation, uninterestedly.*]

Eisaku: But is your husband such a bad man?

Yoshiko: Bad!   What do you mean?

Eisaku: Well.........after all, the problem is whether he loves you or not.   Doesn't he love you?

Yoshiko [*indignantly as though her pride was hurt*]:   Oh, yes, he loves me.

Eisaku: Well, if he does, there is nothing to worry about, is there?

Yoshiko: But he said such terrible things to me today.   For instance, he told me to get out if I wanted to, and to have my own way.   I was so mad!

[E*ISAKU and* N*UIKO glance at each other, and each lets out a forced smile.*]

Eisaku: But wasn't that because you said something to him?

Yoshiko: Oh, yes, that's it.

Eisaku: Look there! A man has a peculiar sense of pride, you see. If the wife says something against him, he unintentionally says extreme things because his pride is hurt. The same thing happens to me, too. At times when I am fretting, being unable to write as I wish, and my wife talks some nonsense, I often beat her out of anger, and tell her to get out and do as she likes. Then, suppose the wife gets out? Usually she comes back within two or three days. But you should know that mere chance often plays a great mischief in our lives. Take your case for instance. Sometime when you quarrel you may happen to leave the house in a pet......though you have least intention to part from your husband.

Yoshiko: Dear me! I have enough intention......

Eisaku: Well, you may have some intention. Suppose the wife leaves home thinking that she will go back if she learns that the husband is in a desperate search for her. It is all very well in your case because you have arrived here safe. But just suppose that you met a kind-looking man in the street car, who talked to you agreeably. You were unhappy and lonesome since you left home, and naturally his sweet words would work on you, and you might have a fancy to him.

Yoshiko: For goodness' sake, no. I am not that fickle-minded.

Eisaku: If not, why did you leave your home?

Yoshiko: Dear me! [*She laughs merrily.* NUIKO *laughs too.*]

Eisaku: Anyway, if you once get married, you couldn't be separated so easily. The conjugal relation is the highest destiny in life, you know. Even though they might be tired of each other sensually after living together for five or six years, they will see that still there is true love somewhere at the bottom of their hearts. There are many cases in which wives get out of the house just by trifling misunderstandings, and later by some mistake they are obliged to get divorced in spite of themselves. Now take your case for instance. It was only fortunate for you that you did not meet any kind-looking man in the street car, but how about your husband? Doesn't he go to a café once in a while?

Yoshiko: No, he never goes to such places.

Eisaku: But he may go to a café now to forget things after you have left him. Or maybe to a *geisha*-house?

Yoshiko: Oh, gracious! My husband has never set foot in such a place.

Eisaku: Well then, he has probably gone to

a café as I said. By the way, your husband is very young yet, I guess.

Yoshiko: He is twenty-eight years old.

Eisaku: Why, he is young! Since he is working in a foreign concern, I suppose he is very smart and handsome.

Yoshiko: Oh, please don't joke......why, yes, ...you make me blush.

Eisaku: But he is handsome, isn't he?

Yoshiko: Oh my, I am ashamed to tell. Oh don't rub it in!

Eisaku: Look there! If he goes to a café, waitresses will make a lot of fuss over him. Naturally your husband, too, will feel like staying there as long as he can't expect any fun if he goes back to the deserted home. A tall and very winsome girl, probably with a little mole under her eye, which makes her fairer, will come and sit beside him......

Nuiko: Oh my! What a detailed description of a waitress, I should say!

Eisaku: Why, yes, I am just imagining a case.

Nuiko: I wonder if you are. Possibly there is such a girl somewhere?

Eisaku [*to* Nuiko]: You keep quiet. Well then, he will exchange a few words with this girl, and he will find that she understands things more

than he expected. By the way, does you husband
like literature ?

Yoshiko : Yes, immensely.

Eisaku : Now he mentions something about
literature, and to his surprise she can talk on such
a subject pretty intelligently, too. Not like a waitress, she has culture. She is bright and smart. He
feels as if he has met a truly modern girl. Next
day as you don't come back he goes to the same
café again. Gradually, he begins to like her in
earnest. At first he was intending to look for you,
but now he will get over that, because he is so
much interested in the girl. As for you, you also
were thinking of going home if your husband came
for you, but as it is, you will come to give up your
husband and get separated. On his part, too, he
may be so minded to marry the girl that he will
give you up entirely. Now you see......at first
you came out not intending to leave your husband,
but the circumstances may force both of you to
be separated at the end.

Yoshiko [*as though deeply impressed*] : Yes,
that's so.

Eisaku : You understand it, too ?

Nuiko [*stubbornly*] : No, I don't.

Eisaku : What do you say, Yoshiko-san ?
Won't you go home in any case ?

Yoshiko [*low-spiritedly*] : But I told him I

would never come back......

Eisaku: Isn't that just stubbornness? It is the women's side that should give in first.

Yoshiko: But I want to start a new life in Tokyo.

Eisaku: If you are hoping for a new life because you are dissatisfied with your matrimonial life, then you are greatly mistaken. While you live in the country, you may feel that a city like Tokyo is a wonderful place to live. However, that's what we call, " Lamplight, distance or an umbrella makes every woman look beautiful." It is only the distant view that makes you think the different life happier. The day before yesterday, I went to Toyamagahara for a walk and I tried to sit down on the lawn to rest. Then I found the grass under my feet was thin and dirty while a spot a few yards away looked much prettier and thicker. So I proceeded there only to find to my great disappointment that the former spot looked far better than the new one. Life is just the same. From a distance it looks beautiful, but if you stand in it, it is thin and dirty. No matter how thin and dirty it may be, it is our life to be satisfied with where you are, and settle down there. [YOSHIKO *and* NUIKO *are silent.*] What would you say now? Don't you have any intention of going home?

Yoshiko: But I came here with the firm determination.

Eisaku: Is that so? But I think I haven't said anything wrong.

Yoshiko: I know that very well.

Eisaku: Well then, please think it over.

Yoshiko: May I stay with you for a few days until I get a job?

Eisaku [*not very keen about it*]: Why, surely.

Nuiko: Please make yourself at home.

Yoshiko: Nuiko-san, do you know any post-office around here?

Nuiko: Yes, shall I go for you?

Yoshiko: No, that's all right. I will go myself.

Nuiko: Then, go to the left, and turn to the right at the end of the street. Then, to the left for about two blocks, and you shall find a post-office there.

Yoshiko: Left......right......and then left. Is that correct?

Nuiko: Exactly.

Yoshiko: Well, I will go.

Nuiko: Then, I will cook while you're out.

Yoshiko: By the way, will you please put this somewhere? [NUIKO *receives the* furoshiki *and puts it in the closet.*] Good-bye.

Nuiko: Good-bye. [YOSHIKO *exit.* NUIKO *and* EISAKU *look at each other.*] I don't know what to do.

Eisaku: I don't, either. I won't be able to write anything if we have such a guest.

Nuiko: Worse than that! We don't have enough bedding.

Eisaku: I can't do anything when we have a stranger around in this small house.

Nuiko: Does she really mean not to go home?

Eisaku: I wonder. Don't you remember that she boasted of her husband a few moments ago? She felt good when I said he was handsome?

Nuiko: Do you think she still loves him?

Eisaku: Love him? Why, of course. She hasn't the slightest idea of leaving him. It's only an aftermath of a lovers' quarrel.

Nuiko: Maybe so, but it is a great bore for us to have her stay here.

Eisaku: It surely is. Our house is not well provided even for ourselves, to say nothing of accomodations for guests.

Nuiko: What shall I do?

Eisaku: She will go home tomorrow. Probably, she means to go home after she makes her husband appreciate her importance, I suppose.

Nuiko: But I can hardly wait until then. It's such a nuisance.

Eisaku: I was thinking of finishing the story

tonight even if I had to stay up the whole night, but it is no use now.

Nuiko: Well, won't you talk more to her? The story you told a few moments ago was so reasonable. You are a marvel when you talk on such a subject.

Eisaku: Don't flatter me! I meant half of the story for you.

Nuiko: Yes, I thought so, too.

Eisaku: Are you still going to your sister's?

Nuiko: Why.........Yoshiko-san's problem is more serious than mine.

Eisaku: So it is; "Brothers may quarrel, but should unite against the common foe!" [*He laughs cheerfully.*]

Nuiko: Won't you do something, dear?

Eisaku.: But we can't drive her out, eh?

Nuiko: Well, how about this, then? I think she is quite homesick now because of your story a minute ago.

Eisaku: Certainly she is! I have a hunch she went to send a telegram home.

Nuiko: That's right. I thought so, too. Now, my dear, I want to make her more homesick.

Eisaku: How would you do it?

Nuiko: Well......er......

Eisaku: What is it?

Nuiko: I am ashamed to tell......

Eisaku: What's that?

Nuiko: Well, you and I might pretend before Yoshiko-san that we are a very happy couple.

Eisaku: That's impossible! You must remember, we quarreled only a short time ago.

Nuiko: Why, we just pretend, that's all. The idea is to make her envious by showing how affectionate we are, then I am sure she won't be able to stand it, and will go home quickly.

Eisaku: A capital idea! Well, we might try it.

Nuiko: Yes, let's try it. Now I'll cook the rice. When Yoshiko-san comes home, remember we are going to act like the happiest couple in Tokyo.

Eisaku: A bit troublesome, but I will try.

Nuiko: Really? I am so glad!

[NUIKO *goes to the kitchen and* EISAKU *lies down by the desk. Then, the stage is darkened for a few minutes to indicate the lapse of about four hours.*

When the stage lightens again, we see a bed in the four-and-a-half-mat room and YOSHIKO *sleeping in it. The sliding door is closed.* EISAKU *sits against the desk in the six-mat room.* NUIKO *is removing the lining from a* kimono *beside him. They force a smile looking at each other.*]

Eisaku [*very tenderly*]: Nuiko.

Nuiko [*very coquettishly*]: Yes, dear.

Eisaku: Won't you help to rewrite these manuscripts?

Nuiko: Why, certainly! Nothing pleases me more than to be of even a little service to you, my dear.

[NUIKO *receives the manuscripts, and finding them all blank, she almost bursts out laughing.*]

Eisaku: Wait, darling. Isn't that pen hard to write with? Use this one.

[EISAKU *picks up a gimlet from the inkslab and hands it to her.* NUIKO *tries hard not to break into laughter.*]

Nuiko: Thank you, dear. Then I shall borrow this fountain-pen. I am afraid of spoiling it, though.

Eisaku: That's all right, darling.

[YOSHIKO, *evidently unable to sleep, turns over on her side.*]

Nuiko: Say, dear.

Eisaku: What, honey?

Nuiko: Won't you take me to Tamagawa sometime soon when you are free from your work?

Eisaku: Surely.

Nuiko [*forgetting that she is only playing*]: Really? will you?

Eisaku: What?

Nuiko: You are not lying?

Eisaku: Of course not. [*Winking at her husband,* NUIKO *tries to make it sure if he really means it.*] Nonsense !

[*Both burst out laughing.* YOSHIKO *turns over again, unable to sleep.*]

Nuiko: Now, dear.

Eisaku: What, darling ?

Nuiko: I want to have one *meisen* dress.

Eisaku: Why, I will buy one for you any time.

Nuiko: The *meisen* silk is greatly improved now, and there are some which look almost like *omeshi* and *kinsha.*

Eisaku: Well then, we shall visit Matsuzakaya Department-Store sometime and buy it for you. But dear, we may as well buy *omeshi* if you like.

Nuiko [*forgetting that it is all make-believe, she is glad in earnest*]: Why, of course, *omeshi* is far better than *meisen.* Will you buy me that ?

Eisaku: O. K., honey !

Nuiko: True ? I am so happy !

Eisaku [*realizing that he would get in trouble afterwards if he went too far*]: By the way, didn't you say once you needed a jade buckle, dear ?

Nuiko: No, I haven't said anything like that.

Eisaku [*with a forced smile*]: Is that so ? I thought you wanted one.

Nuiko: Well, will you get me one, then ?

Eisaku : I was thinking of buying it for you with a royalty I will get from the Yobunsha publishers for my next book.

Nuiko : I am so happy, my dear. You won't forget it, though? [*Meanwhile* YOSHIKO *tosses about, but finally as if unable to stand it any longer, she sits up in the bed and lifts her head.*] If only we had a child, really there would be nothing I would ever miss.

Eisaku : Why?

Nuiko : Well, you love me so much, don't you? [*At this outspoken remark of hers,* EISAKU *tries hard to check his laughter.*] That's what I always believe. You are so good to me, and if only we had children, then I would think myself the happiest wife in Tokyo.

[EISAKU *is a little abashed and cannot chime in with it.* Yoshiko *cannot endure it any longer and lets out forced cough.*]

Yoshiko : Ahem, ahem!

Nuiko [*half to her husband and half to* YOSHIKO]: I am so sorry. Are you still awake?

Yoshiko : Yes, what time is it now? [*She sits up on the bed.*]

Nuiko : It's only ten minutes to ten.

Yoshiko : How long will it take to go from Shinjuku to Shinagawa?

Nuiko [*pokes* EISAKU *and subdues the impulse*

to laugh]: Not more than forty minutes, I suppose.

Yoshiko: Do you think there is a *rikisha* from here to Shinjuku?

Nuiko: Yes, there is.

Yoshiko: Then, I will go home.

[EISAKU *and* NUIKO *do their best to stifle their laughter.*]

Eisaku: Why, that's fine. I quite agree with you.

Nuiko [*laughing relievedly*]: That's a good idea.

Yoshiko: Yes, I will go home. My husband loves me very much, too!

[*Again* EISAKU *and* NUIKO *withhold the impulse to laugh.*]

Eisaku: I believe he does. It is certain that your husband will come for you sooner or later, but it would be much better for you to go home now.

Nuiko [*opening the sliding door*]: Shall I go and call the *rikisha*-man, then?

Yoshiko: Yes, please.

[NUIKO *goes out and* YOSHIKO *dresses in haste.*]

Eisaku: Please give my best regards to your husband. All husbands can't but love their wives so long as they are reasonably good and virtuous. There would develop an inseparable intimacy as fellow beings since a husband and his wife live together under the same roof day in day out. How could the true love in each other's heart die away so easily, even though they may offend each other's feelings for a time? I hope you would try never to let such a thing happen again but live happily.

Yoshiko: Thank you so much. Only half a day from home makes me well appreciate the good in my husband.

Eisaku: Oh, yes; oh, yes. [NUIKO *comes back*.] Is there a *rikisha*?

Nuiko: Yes, I came home with it.

Eisaku: Well then, ride on it quickly. It isn't very good to keep away from home even for one night.

Yoshiko: Then I will be going at once.

Nuiko: Please ride on it.

Eisaku: Be sure that you bring your husband next time.

Yoshiko: To be sure, I will visit you with him to thank you. He has been saying he would like to call on you sometime.' [*Then, at the door.*] Please give me the *furoshiki* which I asked you to keep away sometime ago.

Nuiko: Oh, that! I have almost forgot it.

[NUIKO *hands it to her, and* YOSHIKO *exit. From outside comes the sound of a* rikisha, *and the exchange of " good-bye ".*

Nuiko *and* Eisaku *return to the six-mat room.*
Nuiko *holds her sides with laughter.*]

Eisaku : What's so funny ?

Nuiko : Don't you see how wonderfully my scheme worked ?

Eisaku : Nonsense ! If Yoshiko-san hadn't come, you would have left me.

Nuiko : Yes, that is so.

Eisaku : As we say, "A peace-maker is the savior of the moment," Yoshiko-san is the savior of the moment for us.

Nuiko : But we, too, acted as peace-makers for her, didn't we ? We are the saviors for Yoshiko-san.

Eisaku : Well, that's right. Now, you see how even Yoshiko-san is treated in her own cousin's home ?

Nuiko : Yes, I see.

Eisaku : Yoshiko-san is surely naïve to be so taken in by our trick and to go home so quickly. Women should be of a pliable disposition.

Nuiko : I am quite sure her husband loves her. Wasn't she boasting of her husband when she had left home after having a quarrel with him ?

Eisaku : Anyway, it was all so funny.

Nuiko : It certainly was !

[*Suddenly a bang is heard at the entrance, and they are surprised.*]

X X: I am the *rikisha*-man.   I came to change the *furoshiki* of your guest.

[NUIKO *goes to the entrance in a flurry.*]

Nuiko: Heavens!   I gave her mine.   [*Opening the closet in a hurry,* NUIKO *hands another* furoshiki *to the* rikisha-*man.* EISAKU *is laughing mischievously.* NUIKO *comes back beside him.*]   For goodness' sake!   What a disgrace it would have been if my *furoshiki* had been taken to Yokohama!

Eisaku: There, you see!   You made such a mistake because you were so anxious to leave home.   Lucky it was a small matter like the mistake of the *furoshiki*.   But what would you do if you made a bigger, irreparable one?

Nuiko: I shall never make the same mistake.

Eisaku: No matter how we fight sometimes, we should stick to each other.

Nuiko: But......you don't love me at all?

Eisaku: Yes, I love you.

Nuiko: Would you be always nice to me as a few moments ago?

Eisaku: Why, to some extent, yes.

Nuiko: Well, is that true that you said you would buy an *omeshi kimono* for me?

Eisaku: Nonsense!   That was only in the play.

Nuiko :   Oh, no, I didn't take it that way.

Eisaku :   Well then, I will buy you a *meisen* kimono.

Nuiko :   But didn't you say after all *omeshi* was preferable ?

Eisaku :   You told me that *meisen* was just as good as *omeshi*, though ?

Nuiko :   What a man !   How could you remember such a trifle, dear ?   Well, *meisen* will do just the same.

Eisaku :   I feel so relieved now, that I think I can write the story tonight.

Nuiko :   Please write, dearest.

Eisaku :   Yes, darling.

[EISAKU *goes to his desk, and* NUIKO *opens the* furoshiki *and......*]

— *Curtain* —

THE PASSION
BY SANEATSU MUSHAKOJI
A PLAY IN FOUR ACTS

"THE PASSION"

A PLAY IN FOUR ACTS

By Saneatsu Mushakoji

Translated by Noboru Hidaka

Characters : *Eiji Nonaka* ....29 years old
Chiyoko Nonaka ...25 years old
Shinichi Nonaka ...36 years old
Onodera
Yoshiko, his wife

ACT I

SCENE I

[EIJI's *room. About one o'clock in the afternoon.*]

Eiji : Don't worry about me. I like to think out my own question by myself.

Onodera : I hope you won't do anything rash.

Eiji : How could I ? Do I look like such a man ?

Onodera: You look so lonesome, though.

Eiji: I won't say I am not lonesome, but is there any living mortal who is not lonesome? Is there any man who doesn't feel as if he is cast out alone in the dark? After all, what should we believe? Even when we can't believe anything, still we won't die. I haven't given myself up yet, for, from now on, I am going to do something very interesting.

Onodera: I feel easy to hear that. Since we are counting so much on your future, it is too much for us to have you die now.

Eiji: It is very nice of you to say that. But I won't die. Though I often think that death might release me from suffering, my attachment to this life is too strong. I feel it is no use doing anything, but all the same, it would be no use doing nothing, either. Wait and see, I will turn out some fine work that shall make you be glad for me.

Onodera: I hope you will.

Eiji: Wonder if I can.

Onodera: I am sure you can.

Eiji: As there is something in me that wants to live, I can't die until I let it live.

Onodera: People are all admiring you.

Eiji: Well, I thought they were laughing at me.

Onodera : There are some people who understand you.

Eiji : But there are more people who do not understand me. I myself don't think the attitude I am holding is always justifiable. But maybe I am too pusillanimous. I wonder if it isn't true that I should be angry. It must be because I am pusillanimous that I am not angry.

Onodera : But we all trust in you; only we fear that you might be disheartened by loneliness.

Eiji : You needn't worry about that. I won't change my own idea according to the way people act towards me. Whatever attitude they may take towards me, I won't think about anything but making myself live. In that respect, I am an egoist. Of course, for a time I suffered, because I suspected it before people did,—though I was half doubtful at first. Thanks to that, I was well prepared when they all found out about it, and I could do without pleasing those curious people. I've got still more courage; I made up my mind once for all. I sympathize with brother and my wife. I think it couldn't be helped. I only have to think of myself being single.

Onodera : I am glad to hear that determination of yours. I am sure they all will feel easy. Now, I must be going.

Eiji : Good-bye. Please give my best regards

to everybody. Also tell them that I want them not to worry about me. However, the only thing that is weighing on my mind is that my elder brother is feeding me ; so, I am often jaundiced in thinking if everybody is despising me that I can't be angry with him. But after all, I'll let them think as they like. And, as a matter of fact, what they say is true.

Onodera : Good-bye, then.

Eiji : Please come again.

Onodera : Thanks.

[*They go out. After a while* EIJI *enters again.* SHINICHI *comes in a flurry.*]

Shinichi : I have something to talk about with you.

Eiji : What is it, brother ?

Shinichi : I wish you would tell me where Chiyoko-san is, if you know.

Eiji : Wasn't she with you ?

Shinichi : She came to my house for a short visit the day before yesterday. I haven't seen her since.

Eiji : She hasn't come back since that very day. I thought she was with you.

Shinichi : Wasn't there anything strange about her ? I am worrying about her.

Eiji : Sorry, I am not her watchman. Legally, I may be her husband, but in reality I am an utter stranger to her. So I tell you, I don't know about her.

Shinichi: She always speaks good of you.

Eiji: She has never spoken good of you in my presence.

Shinichi: Please don't be sarcastic about anything. Of course I may deserve it as I am to blame. But I am really worried today.

Eiji: I respect you, brother, but I know that you are a tactician, too. I can hardly believe what you say. For instance, suppose you have come with Chiyoko as far as the corner of the street, you are a man who could say exactly the same thing you have just said with such nonchalance. So, I can't worry about her in earnest with you.

Shinichi: If you talk like that, I can't say anything. But Chiyoko-san—

Eiji: Oh, please don't call her Chiyoko-san. Of course, there is no wrong in your calling her with *san* if you like it, but only be natural. Because I look upon her as your wife.

Shinichi: Why, let's talk no more about her, then. But you really don't know where she has gone? I can't help feeling that something horrible has happened somewhere; I feel as if she might come in at any moment covered with blood.

Eiji: From under the floor?

Shinichi : I won't say so, but—

Eiji : But you can't deny it, either?

Shinichi : She was afraid of you.

Eiji : It was your wife that she was afraid of.

Shinichi : Do you suspect Tazuko?

Eiji : I don't have any suspicions about what may be under your house. But, indeed, I have never expected to see you so sincerely worried about Chiyoko. I thought she was nothing to you but one woman out of hundreds.

Shinichi : Do I look like such a man?

Eiji : Well, you are a great star of today anyway. You have never been wanting for women, I guess.

Shinichi : I only hope that she is not dead.

Eiji : Do you really think that she might be dead, or killed by somebody?

Shinichi : No, I don't, but I had a very queer dream last night.

Eiji : About Chiyoko? I had almost believed that she was with you all this while.

Shinichi : In the dream, she told me that she was killed by you—in this room.

Eiji : Once I wanted to kill her in this room, but I couldn't do it.

Shinichi : Chiyoko-san told me that once she saw you gazing at a dagger in the middle of the night.

Eiji : Maybe such a thing has happened before. But I can love her for what she is—for all
her faults and everything.   As she acts so naturally
in all circumstances, I don't doubt that she loves
me when she says so.

Shinichi : To be sure, she loves you.   If only
you had been a little more careful in watching
her, we would never have fallen into such a mess.

Eiji : She is not afraid to say anything.   I
don't remember how many times she wanted me
to die.   She used to repeat that a woman can't
enjoy a life of ease until she is widowed.   She
had wished for your death, too.   One time I
feared she might kill me.   But, after all, she is
weak-hearted, and when I would get a small cut
on my finger, she would almost cry and make a
fuss over it as if it were fatal.   She won't be able
to kill herself.

Shinichi : But she was saying that somebody
might kill her.

Eiji : That's a mere conceit of hers.   She
has a way of saying such things.

Shinichi : You think she is living, then ?

Eiji : Surely, I do.   Even if she is dead, you
won't be the least bit troubled ?

Shinichi : Yes, I will.   Don't you care if she
dies ?

Eiji : If she dies, so much the better for me,

I guess. However, she is the only woman I have in spite of her being fickle.

Shinichi: Show me your pictures, won't you?

Eiji: They are all trash.

Shinichi: That's all right, show me.

Eiji: Well, I will show you, then.

Shinichi: Gee, what a great improvement!

Eiji: Is that flattery? Please tell me frankly.

Shinichi: Why, I don't know much about painting, but I can see enough to know that you have improved.

Eiji: Maybe I am doing better bit by bit, but surely it is hard to be a success, isn't it?

Shinichi: That's true with everything. One can't expect to be successful too easily.

Eiji: I think that there must be some flash of genius from the first work. When I saw your *début* on the stage, I just admired you. I am afraid there is no such flash in my works.

Shinichi: It's a thing that comes out all of sudden. I think you can be a success.

Eiji: Well, if I think myself hopeless, I won't do painting. Since I have no chance in any other field, I can't help sticking to it. But I am not a bit sorry that I was born a hunchback. I shall only be a little more humble and do my own work whole-heartedly. Any thought I have of women will be because I don't know myself, I suppose.

Shinichi : That's a poser.

Eiji : In a way, I may hate you, but I do respect you as a genius. I believe that your acting is Japan's pride, and I am glad regardless of all other things. From the bottom of my heart I admire your consistent progress in acting.

Shinichi : I am really happy to hear you say that. It is only you before whom I should like to bow down.

Eiji : Oh, don't say such a thing. Please soar up high in the sky, paying no attention to women. And don't worry about me, either. On my part, even clinging to the ground, I will dig out something from there.

Shinichi : I heartily respect you. On the one hand, we may be enemies, but, on the other, I think we are the best of brothers and respect each other.

Eiji : I have attained to enlightenment, brother; let others do as they like! Don't think you can do with even your wife as you please—what you can do as you please with is but yourself, and that in a limited compass. In the very compass, I will try to be as worthy a man as possible. Look at my hands! They are never stained with blood. I think, Chiyoko is a pitiful careature—so are you and your wife. After all, human beings must have been made that way.

Shinichi: That is a poser.

[*Someone seems to be at the door.* EIJI *goes out, but before long he enters again.*]

Eiji: Won't you lend me a hand?

Shinichi: What is it?

Eiji: I bought an interesting thing.

Shinichi: Is that so?

[*They go out. Meantime, they carry along a big Chinese trunk.*]

Shinichi: Oh dear, what an odd thing!

Eiji: I found it at a second-hand-article dealer's, and I was suddenly tempted to buy it. But I was sorry after I bought it.

Shinichi: It is rather big, isn't it? How much did you pay for it?

Eiji: I paid thirteen *yen*.

Shinichi: It's surely cheap.

Eiji: Now, I hope you will keep your acting good, and let people know the genuine joy of arts. Brother, I feel like painting alone quietly, now.

Shinichi: Well, I'll come again. I must be going now.

Eiji: I will let you know when I get any news about Chiyoko.

Shinichi: It will be enough that she is alive.

Eiji: You can be more honest, can't you? Well, please remember me to your wife.

[*They go out. Presently* EIJI *enters again.*]

Eiji: I won't change my life's price according to other people's attitude towards me.

[ONODERA *enters.*]

Onodera: I came back to get my note-book which I forgot.

Eiji: Is that so? Did you see my brother?

Onodera: Yes, I did.

Eiji: You know him, don't you?

Onodera: I have seen him only on the stage.

Eiji: You won't believe that he is my brother. Really there are many kinds of brothers.

Onodera: But there is some likeness between you two.

Eiji: Isn't it about the mouth?

Onodera: Yes, it is.

Eiji: He resembles mother, and I resemble father. We had a sister, besides, but she died. If I had not been a hunchback, I could have grown a little more comfortably. And I might have been more like him, but now we make an entirely different impression on people. Father and brother used to be compared to a crane, but I to a toad. It is a terrible comparison, yet it is true, isn't it? [ONODERA *does not say anything.*] You can't answer, because it is true? But when I was small,

I would adore him still more, instead of getting angry when people said so. But now I think there is something good in myself, too. Only people don't see it, that's all. It is ridiculous that a man like me suffers from women. Not exactly that I suffer from them, but I can be happy only if I realize my limitation. I have only to do the work that suits me. Even for me, there are many things I can do—[ONODERA *still keeps quiet.*] You might sympathize with me, but I am thankful that I can paint by myself somewhere in my heart. In a way, I seem to be an exceptionally easy-going fellow. Someone is at the door, I think. [EIJI *goes out. He is always waiting for* CHIYOKO's *return secretly. He enters again.*] There's nobody. I heard once that there is no tragedy for a wise man. So I am going to try to be one myself. We can avoid a tragedy if we are not too selfish in demanding anything. So with me. It's only too natural that my wife is not satisfied with me. It was a mistake that she came to my place. That's why we should begin with correcting this mistake. But I am already attached to the beautiful body of my wife. There, the tragedy is apt to happen, but it is nothing if you take things like a philosopher. We have only to be utterly indifferent to things. Of course, it won't go so well as we say. But even if it won't

go so well, we can't pervert the truth—I am still
a hunchback, and still a toad! And still I am
a not much humanized, disagreeable man. But in
painting, I believe the good in me will come out.
I, too, am human ; I have something good myself.
So, when I deal with flowers, fruits, mountains
and waters, I can find a work somewhere in my
heart. Therefore I don't think I am unfortunate.

Onodera : There is a big Chinese trunk.
How did you get it? I did not notice it before.

Eiji : Ah, this? You have reason not to
notice it. Why, it just arrived now. I found it
last night by chance, and I wanted to buy it. Isn't
that a fine trunk? However, after I bought it, I
felt as if I bought something quite unnecessary.
Someone seems to have come?

Onodera : It's only your fancy.

Eiji : Well, maybe so. I thought my wife
came back. My brother is worrying for fear I
might kill her. He may well worry about that, as
I myself can't say that I have never wanted to
kill her outright. But to murder—I can see the
aftermath too clearly ; and to force a double suicide
upon her, I have too much work to do. Yet she
might have run away in fear of being killed by
me. What a fool! Of course, I can't tell that I
might not put an end to her in my sleep without
knowing. But it is a joke. She will come back

at any moment. I don't care a fig for her. What
do you say to playing chess? It's a long time
since we played it last. Come on, I will show
you how much settled I am!

[*They begin to play chess.*]

Scene II

[EIJI's *room.* CHIYOKO *is playing on the*
samisen, *and* EIJI *is singing.* ONODERA *enters.*]

Eiji: I am glad you've come. Chiyoko came
back late last night. After all, it seems that she
didn't forget her home.

Chiyoko: Onodera-san, I am so sorry for
letting you worry about me so much. The fact
was that I suddenly became somewhat afraid to go
home and ran away to Hakone. But I ran out of
money, so I came back thinking it was only too
bad if I got killed, but as he was so glad to
receive me, I really felt relieved.

Eiji: So was I. Suppose she hanged, I
wouldn't be able to sleep in peace. But if she is
around me, I have a hard time to paint.

Chiyoko: Look, how he complains that he
can't paint when I came back after a long time!

Onodera: He doesn't have to be able to
paint, I presume.

Chiyoko: When I begin to think that he is
glad that I am alive, he begins grumbling at once

that he can't paint.

Eiji: You see, she plays the *samisen* all morning!

Chiyoko: Who told me to play it, may I ask?

Eiji: Who was it that made me ask for it, though?......especially when I could finish the picture with another effort? Now I feel free and easy, but I couldn't do it though I tried a little this morning.

Onodera: It will be all right again pretty soon.

Eiji: You mean, if she runs away again?

Chiyoko: I won't, even if you asked me to.

Eiji: Nobody will ask you to do such a thing.

Chiyoko: You won't mind even if you can't paint well?

Eiji: Most likely I shall have a different kind of picture.

Chiyoko: It doesn't make any difference whether I am here or not, so I am discouraged.

Eiji: That isn't true. But you know I can't confine you to a room.

Chiyoko: I wish you would. A woman like me doesn't know what to do by herself, if she be left alone.

Eiji: Poor thing! You can't control yourself, then?

Chiyoko: When I realize it, it is too late.

I've made a mistake. It is just laughable.

Eiji [*not angry*]: You sap!

Chiyoko: Won't you lock me in a room, and feed me with goodies? That would be much easier for me.

Eiji: It won't last for three days.

Chiyoko: It depends on you, I guess. Won't you have some *sake*?

Onodera: No, thank you.

Eiji: How about playing cards?

Onodera: No, not today. I must be going in an hour.

Eiji: Where are you going?

Onodera: I have a date with Yamada.

Eiji: Is that the fellow who writes novels?

Onodera: Yes, he is the one.

Eiji: Do you know him?

Onodera: Yes, I do.

Eiji: Please give my regards to him when you meet him. I remember reading one of his books and that I was deeply impressed by it. But stay here instead of going there. I can't help being happy today, and it is better that we three are here than two of us are left alone. Let's play cards.

Onodera: We have agreed to go to see the play in which your brother is going to act.

Eiji: There is plenty more time for the show.

Did Yamada say anything about my brother?

Onodera: He was speaking very highly of him. He said he has never seen such an open-hearted man.

Eiji: Well, he is a genius at acting, but he is a scamp with women. Man has two incomprehensible natures. I admire his acting no less than anybody, but I can't speak well of his character. But it may be just natural that he becomes like that as he makes such a hit with ladies. If it were possible to kill the hateful side in brother, without killing the lovable in him, I would do it.

Chiyoko: Please stop saying such things.

Eiji: Sure, I will. It would be foolish to spoil things when we are in a good humor. However, there are few brothers as interesting as ours. Though I used to admire him ever since I was a kid, I seem to have always hated him. Well, I will stop. I feel chilly.

Chiyoko: It's because that door is open. Really, you must think of your health. You are so important to me.

Eiji: I won't say that you don't mean it, but the next moment you will wish me to die, I guess.

Chiyoko: It seems that there is an awfully good nature as well as an awfully malicious nature in you.

Eiji: Isn't that the same with you, though? If compared with you, there are few who are not good for something.

Chiyoko: What a nerve!

Eiji: Too bad, that's true. I am just crazy about you, but I hate you more than anybody.

Chiyoko: Aren't you drunk?

Eiji: How could I be? But there is no more *sake*, is there?

Chiyoko: You shouldn't drink too much.

Eiji: But won't you allow me to drink one *go* more? Please go and get it.

Chiyoko: Oh, no, you had better stop.

Eiji: Don't be so hard, but please go and get it. You know I haven't had anything to drink for a long time.

Chiyoko: Well, then. I will go and get it. [*She goes out.*]

Eiji: Now, do you think she is a bad woman?

Onodera: No, I don't.

Eiji: She may not be a good woman, but she is not a bad woman. When I look at her, I often feel like a hypocrite. There is no other girl who would behave so audaciously.

Onodera: You had better put a little more restraint on her, and go out with her instead of letting her go out alone.

Eiji: But not with this hunchback?

Onodera : People won't notice you as it is not so big. What would you care if they did?

Eiji : Of course that doesn't matter, and it doesn't disgrace me, either. Even Æsop was a hunchback, I hear. I am not ashamed to be one. For all that, it is not a good thing to look upon, so I don't like to go out much. And I don't like to restrict anybody's freedom, either. Though I call Chiyoko my wife, I don't think she is, but I think she is my friend. While I will be angry with her if I think she is my wife, I could be grateful if I thought she were my friend. I think of myself as being single. Since I have my own work to do, I don't care for the rest.

Onodera : Nevertheless, you need be a tyrant for your wife's sake. She is a person who can't put restraint on herself.

Eiji : Do you think that other people can put restraint on her?

Onodera : I am quite sure that she wants you to boss her.

Eiji : That may be true. But do you think I have never bossed her? Do you think that she would remain quiet when she is restrained? Do you like to make a wife's watchman out of me? I am already sick and tired of all that. Let come whoever likes to come; let go whoever likes to go away!

Onodera :   Are you satisfied with that ?

Eiji :   What should I do if I were not ?

Onodera :   But a conjugal relation won't be like that, I think.

Eiji :   It depends on people.   A couple who can trust in each other, who can never suspect each other in spite of themselves ; or, a husband who has a wife that always sticks to him even though sometimes she may wish that he would leave her for a short while !—there will be many like that in this world.   But I don't exactly envy them. Both sides have their good and bad points.   Let others do what they will, I will go my own way. That's what I think.   I don't want to force any-body to stay beside me.

Onodera :   Really you have never wanted to ?

Eiji :   Why, you don't understand me very well.   But I can't think that even my own wife is not an independent human being.   Of course, I won't say that jealousy, restriction and compas-sion to some extent are not necessary.   Though I don't think that all these are bad, still I don't think it is necessary to restrict each other so much that we tire of living.   I don't think it bad to realize fully a man's life, free from jealousy and restriction.

Onodera :   Don't you care which side you are on ?

Eiji : No, I don't. It's my conviction that a man who has actually fallen down usually has gained something when he picks himself up, and I think I'm right. I do glorify a peaceful matrimonial life. But I don't think such a unique marriage as ours is necessarily bad, either. It has some interest. Why, she is back? No, it's not she. She should be back by this time, or she might have run away again.

Onodera : Could you be indifferent if she did?

Eiji : There is no reason for me to be indifferent. Sometimes something beautiful is engendered from the fact that one can't be indifferent. Perhaps people will think that I am a most indulgent fool. But I have my own way of living. Suppose she run away, I will think that it isn't so bad as I could continue the painting. Even then, she is late coming home. Wait a little, I will go and see.

Onodera : Is the wine-shop that near?

Eiji : Just around that corner. Say, less than 10 *ken* from here, I guess. [E IJI *goes out*; *but soon he enters again.*] She was talking with my brother at the corner. [*He forces a laugh.*] He is so much worried, thinking that I might kill her. A poor sap! [*Unconciously trying to drink* sake, *he notices the bottle is empty.*] I wish she would have the *sake* sent over here quickly. She

doesn't have to bring it home herself. [*pause*] Can
you really understand me? that I try to be as
cool as a cucumber in such a miserable life?
You won't believe it, if I tell you. Now I will
play the *samisen* and show you how smart I am
at it. [*He takes up samisen.*] Well, what shall I
play? [*He is about to sing some melody.* CHIYOKO
enters.] We've been waiting for you.

Chiyoko: Sorry to be late. As the madam
of the wine-shop liked to talk with me for a
little while—

Eiji: Is that so? It was very fortunate that
you could meet—

Chiyoko: Isn't she rather good-looking?

Eiji: Is she?

Chiyoko: Shall I play something?

Eiji: That'll be fine; but after we drink *sake*.

Onodera: Now I will take my leave.

Eiji: Stay a little longer, won't you? Say,
for another ten minutes, or even for twenty minutes
longer? Sometimes it is dangerous that two people
are left alone. Please stay with us until I calm
down.

Chiyoko: Do you feel unwell?

Eiji: Not unwell, but not exactly well, either.

Chiyoko: If that's the case, you had best stop
drinking.

Eiji: Let's drink, anyhow. Then I shall

sing some quiet sweet ballad that Mr. Onodera may hear it. [*Drinking sake.*] As an old saying goes, "The hero is composed in his breast," so I have my way of training my mind. Oh, how I wish to spend this one day quietly and calmly somewhere in my heart!

[*Taking up* samisen, *he begins to play it.*]

SCENE III

[*Night.* EIJI *is sketching* CHIYOKO *with a pencil*; CHIYOKO *is sewing a* kimono.]

Eiji: It seems that I've got the knack of painting.

Chiyoko: That's good.

Eiji: I've never dreamed that there would come such peaceful days.

Chiyoko: I, too, am quite calm.

Eiji: The storm has passed, I suppose.

Chiyoko: Indeed!

Eiji: Wish it would never come again.

Chiyoko: Do you, too?

Eiji: Yes, I do. And it seems that the painting is also going to turn out all right. From now on, people may begin to buy my pictures.

Chiyoko: Please buy me something when they are sold, my dear.

Eiji: Surely, I will. But I wonder when it will be.

Chiyoko: But I will be happy if you can paint good pictures, even though they are not sold.

Eiji: Why?

Chiyoko: Well, because you will be in a good humor. If you fail in painting, you always become peevish. Really I can't bear your peevishness.

Eiji: I won't be peevish any more. I am wiser now.

Chiyoko: Indeed, you've become composed of late.

Eiji: It seems to me that a man becomes wiser if he once loses all he has. For those who can't remain desperate all the time, it isn't necessarily bad to meet with various sorts of hard experiences.

Chiyoko: You don't care what happens, then? That we can't have a child will be all right, too; and that I come back will be all right, too, for you, I guess.

Eiji: I wish I could be like that; that is, if I could cultivate my mind every time I encounter various experiences. But I am no good because I am so quick-tempered. There are times when I don't know what to do with myself.

Chiyoko: Were you really intending to kill me at that time?

Eiji: I don't know what I may do when I

burst into a passion; maybe there is some dreadful blood running within my body. Once I was told that my great-grandfather had killed his own child out of anger by throwing him on a stone because he cried too much. I don't know whether it was true or not. But it's an awful story, isn't it? After that, it was told, he cried bitterly for a long while, talking only about the child. As a matter of fact, I hear that he had loved that one most. There may be a little exaggeration in the story, but I am sometimes horrified when I think the same blood might be running in me. I do feel it's mental training for me to fight against the blood.

Chiyoko: It's a taint of insanity, isn't it? Oh, I am scared.

Eiji: That's why brother is afraid of me, and I am afraid of him.

Chiyoko: I feel somewhat nervous.

Eiji: To tell you the truth, it's a made-up story. I just happened to imagine that there might be such a man among my forefathers. I think there is no man who can't be driven insane by some means. The only difference is that some people are more subject to insanity than others.

Chiyoko: Are you rather subject to it?

Eiji: A man like me will be less subject to it, don't you think? You remember that I was staring at the dagger when you woke up the other night. But it was not that I wanted to kill, but I somehow felt like looking at it. It seems that there still remains the blood of a *samurai*.

Chiyoko: It's a hateful blood that remains, isn't it?

Eiji: It may not be because of the blood. Isn't it true that a man is sometimes inclined to have a look at the dagger in the night?

Chiyoko: I wonder. No, I don't think so.

Eiji: Don't you ever want to look in the mirror at night?

Chiyoko: I am a sort of afraid to look in the mirror at night.

Eiji: Don't you ever want to look in it all the more because you are afraid?

Chiyoko: When I talk with you, I begin to feel somewhat uncanny and uneasy.

Eiji: Do you believe in ghosts?

Chiyoko: I don't think there are such things.

Eiji: It seems that you, too, have never committed murder.

Chiyoko: Have you ever committed murder, then?

Eiji: For Heaven's sake, no. But I think that a man who ever did murder would believe in the presence of ghosts, and he would see the figure of the man that he had killed clearly on the walls, at the ceilings, and on the windows and what not—the very figure of the man when he killed him.

Chiyoko: Oh, I feel uncanny.

Eiji: That's why I tell you it is fortunate to kill nobody.

Chiyoko: I wonder what dying is like?

Eiji: It's a deep sleep, I should say—a sleep never to be awakened.

Chiyoko: That doesn't sound so bad.

Eiji: Only if there were no fear for death. The throes of death are just terrible, I think. Since the life in you is so anxious to continue, it won't be easy to die.

Chiyoko: Is it true that to be strangled is easy?

Eiji: Maybe so if strangled quietly by a girl's plump hands, but I don't think it's easy not to be able to breathe.

Chiyoko: I hear my brother was often strangled while he was practising *jujitsu*; and told me that it is rather comfortable after getting used to it.

Eiji: I am afraid he is a liar.

Chiyoko: But I think it's true.

Eiji: It may not be a lie, but I can hardly think it true; I can't think it comfortable not to be able to breathe. It is not a good thing even to strangle a chicken.

Chiyoko: Have you ever seen it?

Eiji: No, I haven't, but—

Chiyoko: What you talk about is all imaginary, I guess.

Eiji: But I don't think it's wrong. What time is it?

Chiyoko: It's eight o'clock.

Eiji: It's early yet. But shall we go to bed earlier to-night lest we should be troubled by any visitor?

Chiyoko: Yes, let's go to bed.

Eiji: Hey, somebody is behind you!

Chiyoko: A-h! [*She screams.* EIJI *laughs aloud.*] You terrible man! Oh, I was so frightened! [EIJI *still laughs aloud.*] There is somebody behind you, too.

Eiji: A shadow, I suppose.

Chiyoko: It looks like a woman.

Eiji: Was it a hunchbacked woman?

Chiyoko: Please don't talk like that!

Eiji: Don't you like even to hear the word " hunchback ? "

Chiyoko: I don't like the idea that you say such things.

Eiji: You don't like it, eh? So you don't hate this figure of mine?

Chiyoko: You needn't make such a grimace

on purpose.

Eiji: You don't mind, do you? It's lots of fun to see you dislike it.

Chiyoko: I should say it's an awful habit.

Eiji: The impression of a cobra isn't so bad—

Chiyoko: I just hate—that taste of yours.

Eiji: Well, it's not like you. I will kill you tonight.

Chiyoko: You should not make such jokes.

Eiji: Be easy; I won't kill you when I say I will.

Chiyoko: Will you kill me when you say you won't?

Eiji: I don't know about that.

Chiyoko: Are you trying to scare me?

Eiji: Well, maybe. I'll forgive you in the morning.

Chiyoko: I am afraid of those eyes of yours.

Eiji: It is true that you are afraid of my back?

Chiyoko: Please don't look so any more; I don't like it!

Eiji [*laughing aloud*]: The hand of death is on your countenance.

Chiyoko: The hand of craziness is on your countenance. Oh, let's stop joking. You know, it'll surely be a calamity if " we knock in jest and it is opened in earnest."

Eiji: Now, come along. We will fight the battle of life and death today!

Chiyoko: Yes, I will go. I am not afraid of dying.

[CHIYOKO *is about to throw herself upon him.*]

ACT II

SDENE I

[ONODERA's *room, furnished in the Occidental style.* ONODERA *is writing something at the desk.* YOSHIKO, *his wife, enters with flowers and arranges them on the table.*]

Onodera: Oh, you have nice flowers.

Yoshiko: I bought them as they were so pretty.

Onodera: Really pretty. After all, autumn-flowers somehow seem sad.

Yoshiko: It's fine weather to-day. Won't you go some place for a walk?

Onodera: I might.

Yoshiko: Would you take me, dear?

Onodera: Of course, I will.

Yoshiko: That's marvellous! Where shall we go?

Onodera: Where would you like to go?

Yoshiko: Any place will be all right with me, if it is with you. How about you?

Onodera: It will be all right for me, too, if it is with you.

Yoshiko: Oh, my dear!

Onodera: In such fine weather, we'll be pleasant in any place if we only go out in the suburbs.

Yoshiko: Indeed. I'll change my clothes and come.

Onodera: They are all right as they are.

Yoshiko: I will change only my *haori*-coat, then. [*She exit.*]

[*After a little while* YOSHIKO *enters.*]

Yoshiko: Let's go out now, before any visitor jams it up.

Onodera: Well, let's go.

[*A maid-servant enters.*]

Maid: Here is mail for you, sir.

[ONODERA *takes it; the maid exit.*]

Yoshiko: From whom?

Onodera: It's from Nonaka.

Yoshiko: What does he write?

Onodera: He thanks me for my visiting him the other day, and also asks me to feel easy as he is all right now, and can paint well.

Yoshiko: That's a wonderful news. Do you think that the Nonaka folk can get along all right?

Onodera: That's what I can't tell.

Yoshiko: To me Nonaka-san looks strange

though I am sorry to speak ill of your intimate friend.

Onodera: I can't say he is not eerie. Though he is a fellow who has lots of good points, his taste is a little bit morbid. There is something uneasy about him. He must be one of those people who think too hard.

Yoshiko: Why can't he take life easy?

Onodera: Even when he drinks *sake* and plays the *samisen* as if he is free from care, there is something gloomy about him.

Yoshiko: Then, let's go.

Onodera: Let's go. But wait a minute until I write a postcard to Nonaka.

Yoshiko: I hope nobody will come during that time.

Onodera: We may as well refuse to stay. We can tell them that we are just going out.

[*The maid-servant enters.*]

Maid: There is a man—Nonaka by name— who wants to talk to you for a little while if you don't mind.

Onodera: So it was Nonaka who came?

Maid: He is not the one who used to come here; but a very handsome gentleman.

Onodera: Then, it must be Nonaka's big brother. Show him in.

Maid: Certainly, sir. [*She exit.*]

Yoshiko: Are you letting him come in?

Onodera: I can't help it, because he is Nonaka's brother.

Yoshiko: I hate him. I wish you wouldn't meet such a Lothario.

Onodera: Why, he is not a bad fellow.

Yoshiko: But I hate him so much.

Onodera: Lucky that you hate him.

[*They laugh merrily.*]

Yoshiko: Oh, you are horrible! [*She goes out.*]

[SHINICHI *enters, ushered in by the maid. The maid exit.*]

Shinichi: How do you do? I am so grateful that you are always nice to my brother.

Onodera: Oh, don't mention it. Won't you sit down?

Shinichi: No, I will come to the point at once as I am in a hurry. So please excuse me if I say anything impolite or offensive?

Onodera: Please speak out without reserve.

Shinichi: It is about my brother. He is a man you know well, and I do trust him, respect him for what he deserves, and no less than anybody do I put hope on his prospects.

Onodera: We really respect him as a man of surpassing genius.

Shinichi: Thank you. I am proud in a way

to have such a brother.

Onodera: Eiji-san, too, boasts of you.

Shinichi: That makes me feel ashamed. As I see something of genius in him, I am so anxious to develop it in some way. But he is quite a character, as you know. At one time he is bright and obedient, at another he is glum and morose. Nowadays his unhappy mood seems to predominate. Don't you think so?

Onodera: Maybe that's right. But I have just got a card from him, and it says that he is quite settled down and can do his work well, too.

Shinichi: Is that so? I feel relieved to hear that. The fact is that I received a strange letter from his wife just before I left home. To tell the truth, I decided to come over here as soon as I got it. She asked me in the letter to talk over the matter with you by all means.

Onodera: Forgive me saying so, but do you think you can believe what she says?

Shinichi: Certainly there may be something morbid about her, but I don't think what she says is altogether wrong. Though brother seems to be suspecting her and me—it can't be helped even if suspected—we haven't gone so deep as he thinks. However, it may be well said that she approached me first, and she loved him because she loved me —as I spoke well of him to her. Now I realize that it was not good. I had neither thought, nor tried to think, how much her nature and his would come in conflict. In the first place I never thought she would be his wife. Yet I was glad for brother when they were crazy about each other and wanted to get married. Well, it may be no use talking of things past. But she says in the letter that she can't but feel as if she will be killed before long, and she asks us to help her out of it. She also writes that he would have to give up his whole career if she died; she says that she doesn't want to die, but she will be killed if she tries to escape, and it will be the same even when she stays with him. She can neither escape nor stay with him; she doesn't know what to do; so she writes, too.

Onodera: That may be true. He was talking as if he were quite a philosopher when I met him last time. I had the impression that a big rock was about to fall down the slope, but that it was being held by a straw-string.

Shinichi: I've been thinking on my way here about what should be done. I think a change of air would do them good. I think that house is not good.

Onodera: I should say so, too.

Shinichi: And I also think that his mood might be changed if his pictures began to be sold even a little. I can bring out money for it, but if you or I had people buy them, he would rather think himself insulted. He hates extremely to be sympathized with.

Onodera: In truth, that stubbornness is a bad habit of his.

Shinichi: Though it may be because of the stubbornness that he can live along and do his work, it's sure a bad thing.

Onodera: Suppose they consent to change their abode, where should they go?

Shinichi: I don't have any place in mind, but some place bright and open, where they couldn't fuss about trifles, but where they could bask in the sun together......

Onodera: Yes, that would be good.

Shinichi: How about Hayama?

Onodera: That would be all right.

Shinichi: Will you please advise him to go there when you meet him next time?

Onodera: Yes, I will. But before I do that, I'll see if I can find a good house to let.

Shinichi: I am sorry to trouble you, but please dispose of the matter as you may think best. If I were a man of leisure, I could go and look for a house myself. But just at present, I am so busy......

Onodera: The other day we went to see

your play and we all admired it.

Shinichi : Oh, I don't deserve such a high compliment.

Onodera : As for the pictures, Jiro Yamada, a friend of mine, may buy some.

Shinichi : Do you know him?

Onodera : I went to the show with him the other day. He was also praising you.

Shinichi : It is an honor for me to be praised by a man like him. I want to put one of his plays on the stage. Please remember me to him when you meet him.

Onodera : He will be glad, too, if you could take up his play.

Shinichi : I leave my brother's affair in your hands. Please help him. I am really sorry to trouble you, but the sooner the better. We've to fix the matter before it's too late.

Onodera : I might go to Hayama at once.

Shinichi : That is too......

Onodera : That's all right as I have nothing to do in particular.

Shinichi : I am truly obliged. If my brother's folk don't get settled down, I can't, either. I have his wife's letter here with me, would you read it?

Onodera : If you don't mind?

Shinichi : No. Because I absolutely trust you.

[ONODERA *reads it.*]

Onodera: Yes, this is a bit too extreme of Eiji.

Shinichi: It is just as if fire and oil came together when two creatures of such strange attraction come near each other. To cap the climax, our family isn't without some trace of insanity, though it hasn't come out for these three generations.

Onodera: Eiji is too delicate and cannot take life easy, I suppose.

Shinichi: Poor fellow! I think there is some exaggeration in what she says, too, but we can't blame her if she couldn't sleep when he sharpened the dagger at midnight.

Onodera: Not a seemly habit, I should say. I'll get the dagger from him next time.

Shinichi: If you would do that, I could really be easy.

Onodera: Then, I'll go to Hayama now.

Shinichi: Indeed, I hardly know how to thank you. Then, I'll see you again.

Onodera: Anyway I will go and see you in a few days. I hope that everything will be all right.

Shinichi: So I leave everything in your hands. Good-bye.

Onodera: Good-bye.

[*They go out.* YOSHIKO *enters and tidies up the room. Presently* ONODERA *enters.*]

Onodera: Now I have decided to go to Hayama.

Yoshiko: Why?

Onodera: If Nonaka stays in his present house, nothing good will happen, so his brother says. I intend to look for a house for him.

Yoshiko: Oh dear, we won't have a walk, then? I'm so disappointed.

Onodera: I will take you to Hayama instead.

Yoshiko: Take me to Hayama? really?

Onodera: We haven't walked on the beach for a long time. I think the moon will be good tonight, so we shall go to the sea-shore and watch it.

Yoshiko: That sounds just wonderful. So I can see the ocean! Are Mr. and Mrs. Nonaka not on good terms?

Onodera: I think it is no matter, but I was told that she is afraid that she might be killed.

Yoshiko: She is a bit queer, isn't she?

Onodera: But there is something uncanny about Nonaka, too.

Yoshiko: He seems to be a little eerie. I suppose such a man would be very vindictive.

Onodera: I don't know, but it couldn't be said that he is of a frank disposition.

Yoshiko: The Nonaka brothers are entirely different, eh?

Onodera: But there would be some likeness between them—if Nonaka were not a hunchback.

[*The maid enters.*]

Maid: Mr. and Mrs. Nonaka.

Onodera: Please show them in.

[*The maid exit.*]

Onodera: Though it is said, "Talk of the devil and he will appear," I feel sort of funny. I hope he didn't meet his brother. [*They go inside to meet the guests, and enter with them.*] Would you please sit down?

Eiji [*to* CHIYOKO]: You had better sit down now.

Yoshiko: Please sit down.

Chiyoko: Thank you.

[*They all sit down.*]

Eiji: My brother came here just now, didn't he?

Chiyoko: That's impossible, isn't it?

Eiji: Stop making a sign! Does he come here often?

Chiyoko: He saw a man, who resembled his brother so well, turning around the corner of the street just now, and he insists that it was his brother. But I am telling him that can't be possible.

Eiji: You don't have to make such an excuse. I hope that Onodera and brother will be good friends. I can almost see why he has come to your place. So please tell me without reserve —why has he come?

Onodera: He was so much worried about you that he came.

Eiji: About me? Well, that doesn't matter. What was he worrying about?

Onodera: He was wishing that you would live in a much brighter and more comfortable place.

Eiji: It's just like him to think something like that. And you agreed with him, I guess?

Onodera: Surely, I did.

Eiji [*jokingly, but still ironically*]: Then, after all, where was it decided that we should live?

Onodera: We wondered if there were not a proper place somewhere between Hayama and Miura.

Eiji: I thank you for your kind intentions, but I will not leave that house for the time being. The bare thought of moving is unbearable. And I wonder if it is good to go away to a lonesome place......

Onodera: But I think it wouldn't be so bad to leave Tokyo.

Eiji: If that's the case, you yourselves had

better leave Tokyo. I don't want to leave Tokyo.
Besides I don't want to have brother worry abóut
such matters. I am well satisfied with the present
house, and even my wife has a great liking for it.
That's right, eh ?

Chiyoko : I can't say that I have such a great
liking for it.

Eiji : So you like Hayama better ? you like
a place where there is no house around, and
nobody would hear however much you cried and
screamed ?

Chiyoko : But, to be sure, we can be open-
hearted.

Eiji : Whatever you may say, I don't want
to go—though you are at liberty to go alone.

Chiyoko : I can't live in a house alone.

Eiji : Yes, you can.

Chiyoko : But I am afraid to be alone......

Eiji : But you won't be so afraid as if you
stay with me ? She thinks of me as a murderer.

Chiyoko : Surely not !

Onodera : I should say that it is stupid of
you to think that way.

Eiji : I don't think it's good, but I don't
want to leave the house for the present.

Chiyoko : You were saying that you wanted
to move just the other day.

Eiji : How did my brother happen to know

that, though? [*Quietly as if suddenly he remembered something.*] You wrote a letter to him, I presume?

Chiyoko: No, I didn't.

Eiji: As it's unpleasant to show you folks that there is some secret between us, I won't talk about it any more—though I am not ashamed to let you know it. I don't like to touch on other people's secrets nor do I think my taste good to make them tell lies; but if anyone behaves so brazenfacedly, naturally I am disposed to be sarcastic—though I am trying to bridle my tongue......

Onodera: Your brother didn't say that you wanted to move.

Eiji: Are you another liar? You are more familiar with the matter than I. I am trying to be indifferent to the fact that other people know my wife's psychology better than I do.

Onodera: Maybe it is because your nerves are more sensitive than the ordinary person's, but I don't think it much good. Can't you take life easier?

Eiji: I, too, want to, as I don't like to be a detective. For that respect, I've always admired you though you are in better circumstances; you pretend not to notice even when you have already. Therefore, fools, making light of you, think that you are easy to deal with; but they don't know that there are very few who can ever deceive you.

I do admire you that you can look pleased when flattered and pretend to remain fooled, fully understanding the other's mind; I, too, can assume a calm air in most things, but when it comes to an affair between husband and wife, naturally I ask too much even though I think that a couple is nothing but utter strangers who have happened to get together. It will be no use to conceal anything now, I tell you—as you advised me once, I have decided to go with her whenever it is possible. For it will be foolish to leave myself any room for suspicion.

Onodera: I still think that it is not so bad to go to the sea-shore.

Eiji: I can't sleep when the roar of waves is great.

Onodera: Is that true? I feel pleasant when I hear it. Then, how about going to the mountains?

Eiji: I dislike a lonely place. Besides, it is so much trouble to move; I can't see why some people like to move.

Onodera: Maybe that's right. For I, too, don't want to leave this house, though I sometimes like to go to some place for a short visit.

Eiji: My brother seems to have horrible associations with the house; I heard that he had dreamed that Chiyoko's dead body smeared with blood was discovered under the house.

Chiyoko: Oh, don't! Please stop!

Eiji [*jokingly*]: Not a very good dream, but I hope, too, that nothing of the kind will ever happen.

Onodera: Say, that kind of joke is not good.

Yoshiko: You shouldn't say such a thing even in joking.

Chiyoko: He finds joy in saying such things to scare people. And he finds pleasure in imagining a case in which he invites his brother to his room with the trunk he bought the other day, to let him sit on it and then surprise him by suggesting that my dead body is inside.

Yoshiko: That's terrible!

Chiyoko: Sometimes I feel as though such a thing was really taking place and my body was put in the trunk.

Yoshiko: Oh, dear me!

Onodera: Truly, it is not good taste.

Eiji: Maybe an actor's blood is running in me as in brother.

Onodera: Probably it might be good for a movie story.

Eiji: I've never seen movies. Suppose the dead body were not inside the Chinese trunk, but that there were all kinds of good eats and *sake* instead? it won't be bad just to frighten him and see what kind of face he would make—such an experience may serve him in good stead for his acting in the future.

Onodera: Maybe interesting as a *kiogen*.

Eiji: If you agree, too, won't you play a minor part in it?

Onodera: If you are in earnest, I wish you would never do such a thing.

Eiji: I am not serious about it yet. Chiyoko, why don't you ask Yoshiko-san to go shopping with you?

Yoshiko: Where are you going? I'll accompany you.

Chiyoko: Then, please take me with you if it is not troublesome to you.

Onodera: As it is fine weather, you will enjoy going out. And please buy some fruits for me if there are good ones when you come back.

Chiyoko: Now, excuse us for a little while.

Yoshiko: We'll be back soon.

Eiji: Thank you for your trouble. [*Exeunt* CHIYOKO *and* YOSHIKO.] Now, my dear friend, Chiyoko has become such a darling to me lately; I've been afraid to love her until now, for if I loved her I would suffer when she ran away; I've thought of ceasing to love her to such a limit that I wouldn't suffer if she ran away. But, in these few days, suddenly I've come to think that I don't want to lose her at any price. I'm so much troubled.

Onodera: No need of being troubled like that.

Eiji: Yes, I didn't mind the flaw while I was thinking that the stone was of no value, but the more I do love the stone the more have I come to mind it. In spite of the fact that I am very aware that I could have her because of the flaw, this torments me more and more. And, nowadays, I have come to hate brother more than before and to be afraid of him. He hasn't forgot her; and she loves him, too.

Onodera: I think not.

Eiji: Yes, I'm quite sure of it. I can't doubt their love. As I step in between them, they go on loving more and more. Though both of them are afraid of it, they have no help for it. She is not afraid that she may be killed, but she is anxious to escape from me in some way, while he is only worrying if she may die, and wanting to make her live by any means. As I understand that feeling of his too well, I am afraid. If I can do with losing her, nothing will happen. But I positively don't want to lose her. These days I've become wholly restless. I can scarcely tell how many times I wake up in the night, frightened in a dream that she has run away. You can't understand how miserable I feel on such occasions.

At last I've become a man in hell. However much I may, in a more refreshing mood, desire to live alone, I am powerless ; and jealousy and hatred often torture me as if they will burst open my heart. And I don't know what to do. I am restless, and at last I've degraded myself to as much as her warder, and I can't help it. I have but three ways to defeat it ; that is, to kill her, or to kill brother, or to kill myself. Which of these three shall I choose ? It may be I who should die, but who would take up my work if I died ? I can't die for my work's sake. I think of killing brother, too, but people will soon find out that I am the murderer. I wouldn't be able to deceive them by saying that he is traveling ; I don't mean to give up my whole career to kill him. And I can't kill her without losing her ; now, I cannot live without her. I can't see what I should do. You won't see it, either, I guess ?

Onodera: How about traveling—she and you ?

Eiji: It will be the same. So long as she believes in escaping, some day she will run away. That is an unmistakable fact—unless they make away with me. The more I love her, the less I can trust her. You who enjoy domestic bliss, having such a virtuous wife, won't ever understand this feeling of mine even if you are a novelist. I've become unable to take my eyes from her even for a moment. I don't like to give the least reason for suspicion. But as I did not like her to hate me, I might have let her steal time to write a letter. You know she is such a smart creature. I don't want to have you take sides with my brother at any cost, for you are the only one I trust; I am afraid of suspicion most; it is a spectre; it makes an appearance where we can't see its real form.

[YOSHIKO *and* CHIYOKO *enter.*]

Yoshiko: We are back, sir.

Eiji: Thank you so much. Did you finish shopping?

Chiyoko: Yes, I did.

Eiji: Well, shall we take our leave?

Chiyoko: Yes.

Yoshiko: Why such a hurry?

Eiji: From now on, we'll come down here often to see you.

Yoshiko: Please do come again.

Chiyoko: Thank you.

Eiji: Now, we must be going.

Onodera: Well—good-bye.

[*They all go out and say "good-bye". Presently enter Mr. and Mrs.* ONODERA.]

Onodera: Certainly this is some trouble.

Yoshiko: Chiyoko-san is a very nice lady,

isn't she?

Onodera: Surely, she is. But she looks some-what ill-favored.

Yoshiko: She was so weakened that her eyes soon glistened with tears. I was so sorry.

Onodera: I should like to help them in some way or other. But, as it is a personal affair be-tween another man and his wife, I don't know how to deal with it.

Yoshiko: I am afraid there is nothing to do but look on them in silence.

Onodera: What do you think? Will Nonaka kill his wife or not?

Yoshiko: I can't tell that.

Onodera: Will she run away before she is killed, or will she be killed before she runs away? I can't tell either.

Yoshiko: I wonder why things cannot come right peacefully, when both of them are such nice people.

Onodera: All three are not bad people, but they are too tenacious of nature if anything. I feel so depressed. Let's go for a walk.

Yoshiko: I've bought some fruit.

Onodera: I had almost forgotten about it. We shall eat it after we come back.

[*As they go out.*]

— *Curtain* —

ACT III

SCENE I

[EIJI's *room. He is painting*; CHIYOKO *is reading a novel, but all of sudden she falls to crying.*]

Eiji: Fool! How can you cry like that, just reading a novel?

Chiyoko: But it is so sad.

Eiji: Maybe because you compare it with your own miserable lot?

Chiyoko: Yes, it is so.

Eiji: So I told you not to read novels.

Chiyoko: If I didn't read novels, I would be more lonesome.

Eiji: Why not do some work?

Chiyoko: Am I not working without keeping a maid-servant? Even if I work harder, it won't mean that we can get some money or we will have any happy prospects for the future.

Eiji: Is it true that you can't have a child?

Chiyoko: The doctor said so. He said that there is something wrong with my womb. I think it's lucky for me that I don't have any children.

Eiji: Why?

Chiyoko: If I had a child on top of this, my health wouldn't last long.

Eiji: Do you wish me to die?

Chiyoko: You like it better that I die, I guess?

Eiji: It's better than to have you escape from my hands.

Chiyoko: I, too, would rather die than to continue such a life as this forever.

Eiji: Before long people will begin to buy my pictures—and pay two or three hundred *yen* for one picture.

Chiyoko: As I am confident that they will never pay even ten *yen* for your picture, I won't believe it even if you say so.

Eiji: Well, wait and see.

Chiyoko: And no matter how rich we may become, I don't like this kind of life.

Eiji: Then, what do you want to do?

Chiyoko: I can't stand such a life that I can't go to any place I wish.

Eiji: It's all because you do such things that I can't trust you.

Chiyoko: I feel sick even looking at your face and figure.

Eiji: At last you tell me the truth, don't you?

Chiyoko: I am not scared of you any more; I had better die than have us shut in such a place as this, unable to go out in this fine weather.

Eiji: Presumably you are wishing me to die sooner?

Chiyoko: Well, maybe. I want to go out

as often as I like. If you only grant me freedom,
I'll surely come back to you. But, if you take
away my freedom as you do, and threaten to kill
me, I can't but be secretly determined that some
day I will manage to run away.

Eiji: Say whatever you like! The snake
will never let go the rat he has seen no matter
how much he may squeak.

Chiyoko: Really you are a cruel man!

Eiji: Which one of us is more cruel?

Chiyoko: Perhaps I was once to blame, but
at present you are the one to be blamed—far more
to be blamed! I do hate you to the core. It is
going too far to restrict my liberty.

Eiji: Do you think that I am fond of doing
that? You should have known how it hurt me.

Chiyoko: As I know it, I have endured
staying with you until now.

Eiji: Do you say that you can't endure it
any longer?

Chiyoko: Even I must live.

Eiji: Even in killing me?

Chiyoko: You are not a man who would
ever die; you won't die even though you may kill
me. You are not a man who could die with
someone for love, even when you could kill me
and laugh at my dying.

Eiji: Yes, that may be so. Suppose I die

now, I won't be able to show anybody that my work can be something. At least I want to leave work that is good enough not to be laughed at by men of understanding.

Chiyoko: You wouldn't care if I were dead, if you could only paint!

Eiji: That's a matter of course.

Chiyoko: Why a matter of course? How mortifying!

Eiji: Cry as much as you can! Nobody is going to sympathize with you!

Chiyoko: I don't want your sympathy. I do not think of you as my husband any longer. You are a tyrant! a terrible tyrant!

Eiji: Did you get that stuff from the novel?

Chiyoko: What's the novel got to do with it? I will leave.

Eiji: Go if you've got enough nerve!

Chiyoko: Surely, I will!

Eiji: Say it once more!

Chiyoko: I'll say as many times as I like! I will go out!

Eiji: What a nerve you've got to say that! [EIJI *is about to jump on her in anger, when* ONODERA *enters*.] I am so glad you have come. Just now, [*Grinning.*] we were quarrelling. I was wishing some one would come.

Onodera: As it is said that " not even a dog

turns at a quarrel between a couple," so I don't like to, either.

Eiji: Well, let it be. But she trifles with me too much—

Chiyoko: Onodera-san, please listen to me. He watches me from morning till night; he won't grant me any liberty whatever. Does a husband have a right to do such things? to deprive his wife of all the joys of life, and to make her obliged to commit suicide?

Eiji: How much I have wished to please you, you should have known it. [*To* ONODERA.] You know it, too, don't you?

Onodera: Yes, I do.

Eiji: For all that, she—she is cursing me, and she says she would rather die than to stay with me. For a husband, would there be a more bitter insult than this? [*He weeps.*]

Chiyoko: How much have I tried to love you, too! But I don't have that power. What you ask is too much!

Eiji: Then, get out!

Chiyoko: Certainly I will.

Onodera: Okusan, you shouldn't say such foolish things!

Chiyoko: But he says, " Get out." I don't want to die here, either.

Eiji: Even I am a man! Get out!

Onodera: You, too, shouldn't say such foolish things. You know that she has no place to go, don't you?

Eiji: There are many places she can go. She picked a quarrel with me because she has already found a place to go.

Chiyoko: No, that's a lie! I don't care for any place to go.

Eiji: When you have no place to go in your mind, are you going out?

Chiyoko: You wouldn't tell me to go out if I had a place to go?

[*They are forced to laugh, looking in each other's face.*]

Onodera: That's why I told you, " Not even a dog turns at a quarrel between a couple." Well, well, I don't know which one of you is to be blamed, but both of you should give in.

Eiji: How could I give in?

Chiyoko: I won't, either.

Onodera [*laughing aloud*]: That's fine. Go ahead and fight more!

Eiji: Now that we have such an interrupter as he, I may give in; so won't you bring some tea?

Chiyoko: Yes, I will.

Eiji: Shall I show you the chrysanthemum which I bought the night before last?

Onodera: Yes.

[*Exeunt* EIJI *and* ONODERA.]

Chiyoko [*aside*]: Ah, ah! When I could all but escape from all this, I was caught again in the spider's web.

— *Curain* —

SCENE II

[*The same room. An afternoon, several days later.* CHIYOKO *is sweeping in the room alone.* EIJI *comes in.*]

Chiyoko: How was it?

Eiji: Oh, there were wonderful pictures. Though these days I've been despairing of my ever becoming an artist, still when I see good pictures I think that after all there is no other work so happy and so fine as an artist's. I have never enjoyed looking at pictures more than today. There may be really excellent painters in China, but Japanese artists are not so bad, either. For instance, two pictures by Sesshiu which I saw today were truly excellent, as might have been expected. It was the first time that I've ever seen such good pictures even by Sesshiu. If I had had money, I would have bought them. If I had bought them, I thought that they would serve as very good stimulus to my work. If brother were in Tokyo, I would recommend them to him. Too bad that he is in Hokkaido. A painter is lucky as his value is known universally in a short time, and there won't be any lies when his work is known to posterity. Did anybody come in my absence?

Chiyoko: No, nobody came.

Eiji: I should like to be a great artist. Now, I want to paint the mountains. How I wish to travel! How much money have you?

Chiyoko: I've saved up—about thirty *yen*.

Eiji: I'll give you some credit for that. But is it your preparation to run away?

Chiyoko: I've given up the hope already. And besides there would be no place to go.

Eiji: Can I have that thirty *yen*?

Chiyoko: Surely.

Eiji: Then, shall I make a journey and paint the mountains?

Chiyoko: Yes, you had better—even for your health.

Eiji: How about during my absence?

Chiyoko: I will ask my brother to come down over here.

Eiji: That will be fine. I shall go tomorrow, then.

Chiyoko: So sudden?

Eiji: You know, "There is no time like

the present." Now, I will go to Onodera's and make him glad by showing him that I am in high spirits.

Chiyoko: He will feel relieved. Can't I go to his house with you, too?

Eiji: Sure, you can. Come.

Chiyoko: Yes.

Eiji: Now I want to paint pictures whole-heartedly, not thinking about things foreign to my character.

Chiyoko: I am sure you will become a really great artist.

Eiji: How you flatter me!

Chiyoko [*coquettishly*]: But I somehow feel so.

[*They go out.*]

— *Curtain* —

Scene III

[*The same room.* Shinichi *and* Chiyoko *are talking.*]

Shinichi: Don't you get any news from Eiji yet?

Chiyoko: No, I don't.

Shinichi: I wonder how he is getting along?

Chiyoko: He is thinking lots, I suppose. He was wanting to separate from me in earnest. Or else he may be up to the eyes in his work.

Shinichi: Well, I will come around again.

Chiyoko: Why not stay a little longer?

Shinichi: I can't be quite at home in this room with you alone. For Eiji may be back at any moment.

Chiyoko: Don't worry about it. He is actually sick.

Shinichi: He is sick? And aren't you calling to ask after him?

Chiyoko: I don't have any money, even if I want to.

Shinichi: I shall lend you some.

Chiyoko: To tell the truth, I myself am another patient—until the day after tomorrow, I mean while you stay in Tokyo.

Shinichi: I should say that is not good.

Chiyoko: But I can't help it. However, if you insist that I should go to him, I will go even if I die—even I must have some little joy to live. I am really disgusted with staying with him. I know that it is not nice to think that way, but the more I try to love him, the more I feel repugnance for him. I can't put up with it any longer. But you know I have no place to go. And it seems that he wouldn't even stick to his threat to kill me. He is your brother, but he is entirely different, and he is so much attached to me. I am grateful for it, but—

Shinichi : If I hadn't loved you, I wouldn't have such worries. Since our local performances this time made unusual hits, there was one contract after another to be accepted, but I was so much worried about you that I managed to have six days' vacation to come back. As we were just going to the Aomori district again then, they were all against my coming back. But I couldn't listen to what they said.

Chiyoko : Would you cry for me if I died?

Shinichi : I don't want to have you killed. I will do anything to prevent that.

Chiyoko : I often wish I could die with you, but you have never thought anything like that, I guess?

Shinichi : Though I think of living with you, I have never thought of dying with you.

Chiyoko : I never think of living in happiness, —though I did once, when I met you for the first time. I had never been so happy. All sorts of things have happened since then, haven't they?

Shinichi : I have so many things for which I should like to apologize to you.

Chiyoko : No, you don't have anything to apologize for. Because I can live as you are living. And that I have come here was all because I was faint-hearted. It was wrong that I pretended to show that the one I loved was your brother, thinking too much of your home, your reputation, and your popularity. But what is done can't be undone. I don't know about you, but our unhappiness is nothing but the result of a false love; it is a failure of *kiogen*. We can't hold a grudge against anybody for it.

Shinichi: Let's talk no more about such things. I feel somewhat uneasy in this room.

Chiyoko: You are so weak-minded. It is because you are happy. As I am tired of living, there is nothing that I am afraid of.

Shinichi: Isn't Eiji seriously ill?

Chiyoko: No, not very seriously. You needn't worry about him, as I have written to him that I would be recovered from sickness in a few days, and would visit him. You will scarcely understand how happy I was to hear that you came back so suddenly. Anyhow I have been thinking that I could never see you again in my life, as I was with a watchman.

Shinichi: You must think, we are young.

Chiyoko: But I am afraid I can't live long. As it is now, I am really getting tired of living unless the time comes when he can live without me.

Shinichi: Isn't Eiji a good man?

Chiyoko: I know he is. But while I forget

time when looking at the face of such a wicked man as you, I tremble the moment I see his face or his figure. I think there is no greater misfortune for anybody than to live with a grub or a snake in the same room. I didn't take it to my heart so much as that until two or three months ago, but in these days I have a chill come over me even looking at his face. I am not telling a lie. I know that is bad, but everything he does, and every word and every phrase he utters, makes me so sick and tired. I don't know why myself.

Shinichi: Surely, it is a terrible situation. If it were true, you would have to get divorced.

Chiyoko: I think so, too, but what should I do after I got divorced?

Shinichi: It won't be necessary to worry about things after you get divorced. Yet I am a little concerned about when you are divorced.

Chiyoko: If it is only to get separated, I think I can make it in some way or other.

Shinichi: As for me, I can't help thinking how much he will be weakened. I love my brother, though it may be very selfish of me to say that after making him suffer so much—

Chiyoko: He wishes that you would die.

Shinichi: Is that true?

Chiyoko: Yes, it is. Some one of us three

has to die, so he says. And first of all he wishes
for your death.

Shinichi: He may well say so. But I can't
die for him now.

Chiyoko: He was once thinking in dead
earnest of scaring you by making you believe that
my dead body was in this trunk, and he wanted
to see how much you loved me.

Shinichi: He means to have a sort of revenge
on me, I guess. He will be able to play that
kiogen very cleverly. For there is something
uncanny about him, I've often thought that he
would play far better than I do, if we ever gave
him a chance to play such a part on the stage.

Chiyoko: I want to forget everything about
him.

Shinichi: You have grown so skinny, haven't
you?

Chiyoko: I have become ugly.

Shinichi: I really wanted to make you happy.

Chiyoko: My husband says so, too, sometimes.

Shinichi: You are the one who can't forget
him, aren't you?

Chiyoko: The more I want not to think of
him, the more I remember him. Often I wish I
could die. But the more I wish so, the healthier
he gets. I haven't seen such a robust man—strong

to the bone—before. He is such a man who would come to life again and again no matter how many times he might be cursed; I sometimes feel so uncanny. It is just a wonder that you have a brother like him.

Shinichi: Isn't someone coming?

Chiyoko: Only rats are making noise. Nothing to be afraid of. I never thought that I would ever get a chance to talk with you alone. I feel the loneliness which has really frozen at the bottom of my heart gradually melting. When one can be happy like this, must she live in an unpleasant environment day after day?

Shinichi: You shouldn't say such things.

Chiyoko: Today you won't hurry away, will you? I will go and buy *sake* for you.

Shinichi: I must be going home soon today.

Chiyoko: Don't be so hard-headed, please. Because at least to-night I want to be happy. You understand, don't you?

Shinichi: I surely heard some noise.

Chiyoko: Never mind. That is only rats. It is not like you......

Shinichi: I am more afraid of my brother than of anything else in the world. If I see his face, my spirit freezes.

Chiyoko: Mine is always frozen. [*She laughs.*]

Shinichi: It would be intolerable.

Chiyoko: Won't you take me with you on your trip?

Shinichi: How about brother?

Chiyoko: As he is a man, he can live alone.

Shinichi: Yet it is not good to run away when he is sick.

Chiyoko: If I don't run away now, I couldn't ever. Even I don't like to die. If I don't run away now, I will certainly be killed. [SHINICHI *does not answer.*] I don't care to die; I am already desperate; I don't want to stay here any longer even if I die. Please help me! Please let me live! Please don't leave me to fate! [*She bursts into tears on his lap.*]

Shinichi: Oh, don't cry like that. Even I can't get you killed. If your determination is firm, I will make up my mind, too. Surely brother, too, won't go so far as to kill himself.

Chiyoko: Thank you, thank you. Now, indeed I feel relieved. Then, I will pack up my things, so please come to take me tomorrow morning, will you? I shall be through with putting things to rights by that time.

Shinichi: That's all right. I must be going now.

Chiyoko: Well, don't fail to come and take me about nine o'clock in the morning.

Shinichi: No, I won't. So long until tomorrow.

Chiyoko: Oh, I am so happy. I am quite sure I won't sleep tonight. So don't forget about tomorrow.

Shinichi: Now, good-bye.

Chiyoko: Then, I will go with you as far as over there.

[*They go out.* Eiji *enters, and sits on the Chinese trunk, smiling eeriely.* CHIYOKO *comes in in high spirits. She does not notice him first, but soon finding his presence by chance, she screams in surprise. Having a hard time not to faint, and summoning courage, she speaks challengingly.*]

Chiyoko: When did you come back?

Eiji [*coldly*]: Just now.

Chiyoko [*still more screwing up her courage*]: How is your sickness?

Eiji: How about yours? I was so much concerned about it that I forced myself to come back.

Chiyoko: It was so nice of you.

Eiji: Are you glad for my coming back?

Chiyoko: It is understood without saying so.

Eiji: How is it understood?

Chiyoko: Just as you like it.

Eiji: How much do you think I was worried to receive a telegram that you were sick? How earnestly did I pray to God that you might recover! And I was so much worried about you that I came back straining myself. And what do you think I was shown?

Chiyoko [*calmly*] : I, too, want to live.

Eiji : Do you want to live even in cheating me? Why don't you talk more frankly?

Chiyoko : Because I can't think that you would let me go even if I told you the whole truth.

Eiji : Did you call in brother?

Chiyoko : No, that isn't true. Shinichi-san suddenly came back from the journey, as he was so much worried about me. But I had a hunch that sooner or later this day would come. And I was waiting for it, too.

Eiji : So you don't care a fig for me?

Chiyoko : You are a man who can live by yourself.

Eiji : I think you don't have to run away when I am ill.

Chiyoko : I knew that your illness was a feigned one, too.

Eiji : No, mine was not.

Chiyoko : But you asked me to come over as you couldn't travel. Wasn't that a lie?

Eiji : The doctor told me to stay still, but on reading the telegram that you were sick, I feared you might die......

Chiyoko: I wouldn't die unless you came back.

Eiji: I thought you were lying in the sick bed alone.

Chiyoko: You came back because you heard from some friend of yours that Shinichi-san was back, isn't that right?

Eiji: Blockhead! That is a lie.

Chiyoko: But weren't you wishing me to die? [*She weeps.*]

Eiji: Cry as you like! Nobody will sympathize with you if you cry! Now I read your mind full well.

Chiyoko: Then, let's get divorced without any ill-feeling.

Eiji [*coldly*]: I would, if you would swear to break up with my brother.

Chiyoko: How can I know about such a thing in the future? [*They stare at each other in silence.*] I am not in the least scared even if you make a face like that.

Eiji [*starting*]: So you are intending to separate from me?

Chiyoko: There is nothing else for me to do.

Eiji: Do you think I will approve?

Chiyoko: No matter whether you approve or not, I've decided to go.

Eiji: Even when I don't agree to it?

Chiyoko: Yes.

Eiji: Try to go out! I have tried to forgive you as much as I could, and wanted to understand your feelings as much as I could. But now I can no longer stand your insult!

Chiyoko: What do you mean to do if you can't stand it? Do you mean to kill me? Do you think you could live peacefully by killing me? You don't mind going to jail, do you? You don't mind having people laugh at you, do you? Or else, are you thinking of committing a double suicide? When you consider what would happen after my death, do you still think you would like to kill me? [EIJI *does not answer*.] Does a wife belong to a husband? Is she his slave and can he kill her? And do you think it is his right to threaten his wife by telling her that he would press her in the trunk and kill her if she ever tried to escape? How much I, too, wanted to love you! But as God hasn't allowed that, I couldn't do anything about it. I think there is no help for it. Of course, sometimes I have felt very sorry for you. But I have made up my mind; I will take my leave now. Please take good care of yourself.

[CHIYOKO *is about to go out quietly.* EIJI *who was looking after her malevolently for a little while, finds her attitude unbearable, and jumps on her. He beats her like a crazy man. At last* CHIYOKO *defies him. Meanwhile he strangles her as if he has gone crazy; she is dead; still strangling her for a while, he laughs hysterically. Presently he stands up.*]

Eiji [*gazing at the dead body, in a low voice*]: What I have done was unavoidable. I couldn't do anything but this. You deserved death! Anybody will think what I have done was justifiable. Die in peace! [*Walking around the room uneasily, he shakes and claps his head madly, and stops before the corpse and stares at her dead face. He suddenly cries out. In a low voice.*] You have been such an unfortunate—unfortunate woman! I wanted to make you happy! But I couldn't do anything else. Namu-Amida-Butsu, Namu-Amida-Butsu—

[*Abruptly he clings fast to her dead body, and suddenly with a keen desire to bring her back to life, he tries an artificial respiration, and he is all the more flustered.*]

— *Curtain* —

ACT IV

Scene I

[*Next morning, the same room. Eiji walks around in a restless manner, bows down before the trunk, almost touching his head on the mat, and tears his hair in agony. There is heard* SHINICHI *calling " CHIYOKO-SAN " from outside.* EIJI's *attitude is suddenly changed, and he sits on the trunk.*]

Shinichi: Chiyoko-san! [*He comes in calling her name. He stands face to face with* EIJI.]

[*Pause. They try to look into each other's heart.*]

Eiji: She went out early this morning. I thought she went to your house. [*pause*]

Shinichi: When did you come back?

Eiji: When did you come back, brother?

Shinichi: A few days ago.

Eiji: I came back late last night. I didn't have even an inkling that you were in Tokyo, as Chiyoko didn't tell me anything.

Shinichi: That's why you thought she came to my house?

Eiji: The moment I heard your voice, I thought so. Didn't she go to your place?

Shinichi: No, she did not come.

Eiji: Is that true?

Shinichi: It seems that you are smarter lately in telling lies.

Eiji: But I am no match for you in acting.

Shinichi: I wonder. About when did she go?

Eiji: About six, I think.

Shinichi: What did she say when she left?

Eiji: She said she was going just over there, but she is not back yet.

Shinichi: Is that true?

Eiji: Well, maybe. Anyhow Chiyoko is not at home.

Shinichi: Is that so? [*He goes out, but presently comes back.*] But there are her *getas*. [*"GETAS" are Japanese wooden shoes.*]

Eiji: She might have gone with another pair of *getas* on. Surely she wouldn't go barefooted or with only *tabis* on.

Shinichi: You did not sleep last night?

Eiji: I am sick, though not so seriously.

Shinichi: That is too bad.

Eiji: Though I have been prohibited by the doctor to travel, I hurried back in surprise on getting a telegram that Chiyoko was sick. But the journey was much better for my health. It seems that my sickness doesn't grow worse a bit.

Shinichi: Was Chiyoko-san sick?

Eiji: Don't you know that? She says she is all right now, and as she got up early in the morning and went out, she couldn't be so sick.

Shinichi: She was fearing you would kill her.

Eiji: Perhaps because she had a guilty conscience.

Shinichi: What sort of woman do you think

she is ?

Eiji :   That is what I want to ask you. But I don't think she is a bad woman, though I think she is too honest. It seems to me that man should not be too honest.

Shinichi :   Was it too late?

Eiji :   What is it?

Shinichi :   I had wanted to have Chiyoko-san live.

Eiji :   She is not dead.

Shinichi [*so glad*] :   True?   Surely, you wouldn't tell a lie about that?

Eiji [*laughing aloud*] :   Did you think I've killed her?

Shinichi :   Why, I can't but think so.

Eiji [*still laughing aloud*] :   You think that Chiyoko deserves to die? Do you think I can commit murder?   I feel I've often been a part of such a scene as today's. [*Changing tone.*] She is a little late coming home.

Shinichi :   Did she go out after a quarrel or something ?

Eiji :   We had a quarrel; she was not glad a bit even when I came back, and she looked rather annoyed. So naturally I did not feel good, and I said something harsh and did something violent. But I frequently go into such rages, so I think she is not frightened away for good.

Shinichi: Don't you have any idea where she went?

Eiji: No, I haven't. She may have carried twenty or thirty *yen* with her. She could have gone a long way. But she will come back.

Shinichi: Forgive me. I thought you really killed her. Thank goodness that she is alive! I don't know how to thank you. When I saw your face, I was struck with terror. I thought it was too late. I did not know what to do.

Eiji: I believe you are trying to take her away from me.

Shinichi: No, that isn't true. I won't say that I don't love her, but I was afraid that she might die. As she wrote me so often that she might be killed, I couldn't help feeling uneasy about her. Since it was I who found you Chiyoko-san, I feel responsible for her, and I wouldn't like to make a murderer of you, either. It would indeed be intolerable if you became a murderer. Of course, I don't think you would do such a thing, but I was frightened when I saw your face a moment ago.

Eiji: But it was because you came in calling Chiyoko's name when you were supposed to know that I was absent.

Shinichi: I am sorry—very sorry for it. I had some kind of bad dream last night—though I forgot the dream—and I was so much concerned about it—

Eiji: Brother, haven't you ever wanted to die ?

Shinichi: You shouldn't die, though.

Eiji: Have you never wanted me to die ?

Shinichi: How about you ? I think you have wanted my death.

Eiji: The same with you, I presume. Brother, what in the world do you suppose death is like ?

Shinichi: I don't know much about it.

Eiji: If one died, would he be happy or unhappy ?

Shinichi: Whosoever has already died will be happy.

Eiji: What do you mean ?

Shinichi: For he won't have to die twice.

Eiji: Do you think so, too ? that those who are dead are happy ?

Shinichi: But I don't mean that murder is good or suicide is good, because as a matter of course living mortals don't like to die.

Eiji: But I think that those who have already passed the barrier of death are in peace. Though it is natural for the living to want the dead to come back to life, it seems to be a misplaced kindness for the dead.

Shinichi: But if he came back to life, it is human that he should be glad about it.

Eiji: It will be so after he has lived again, won't it? Sometimes I envy those who are dead and can never come back to life.

Shinichi: Chiyoko-san seems to be back?

Eiji: What do you want her for?

Shinichi: Well, I just thought she was back.

Eiji: She will come back pretty soon, as she was saying that there was something that she should attend to about nine o'clock.

Shinichi: Is that so? Why, it's almost ten.

Eiji: I wonder where she went. She will be back very soon, I hope.

Shinichi: Is it true that she is alive?

Eiji: You are so doubting!

Shinichi: For there is something I don't fully understand in your expression. You are an honest man and your expression used to accord with your speech, but today they are not in harmony.

Eiji: It is because you don't know what feeling I have towards you. I do hate you, and none the less I love you. I do despise you, but none the less I do respect you. To be frank with you, I don't like to see you, and yet I am concerned about you. I hate that you are here, but if you should go away, I should like to have you stay with me. I fear that you might meet her somewhere. It is no wonder that my expression is not in harmony, for you came back hurriedly in my absence.

Shinichi: I didn't know that you were away from home.

Eiji: Is that true?

Shinichi: Yes, it is.

Eiji: But there is no denying that you entered the room in my absence, is there? You couldn't say that you didn't come in here knowing my absence and that you were not afraid I might come back? When I imagine things like that, I feel my body cut into pieces. Man and woman, husband and wife, the feeling that absolutely abhors to be interfered with by others! You don't understand these things, I fear? I hate your way of thinking that everything would be all right if you wiped your mouth after you stole in the house like a robber-cat. Especially when you have the same blood as mine, it is all the more unbearable. Of course, I don't think jealousy is a good thing, but I am afraid you have not a little to answer for, making your own flesh—and that of your crippled brother—jealous. Say, brother, don't you think so? I have wanted to talk about lots of things to you for once without reserve. But as I did not exactly get hold of any fixed evidence, and as I also thought it shameful for a man to suspect such a thing, I have stood as much as I could. Will you please fully understand this feeling of mine? [SHINICHI *does not answer.*] Brother, you called me a murderer, eh!

Shinichi: I didn't say that.

Eiji: You said so a few moments ago!

Shinichi: I only said that murder is not good.

Eiji: Is adultery good, then? I say, adultery!

Shinichi: Will you please stop threatening me like that?

Eiji: Your punishment can't be called heavy, if it is compared with the pain I have suffered mentally.

Shinichi: Say whatever you like. If you act like that, I, too, will talk frankly. I gave up Chiyoko-san as I sympathized with you, and that was the greatest blunder I have ever made. I found the girl I love for a man she doesn't love. It was the greatest crime I have ever committed; the other crimes are nothing but their natural consequences. You should have known that. For all that, you wanted to get married to her. So, that was your crime as well as your punishment. It is not good that two men love one girl; that's why I found her for the man she didn't love. Do you know which is the more crime, that we two men love the same girl or that I find her for the man she does not love? I may be a libertine, but, I have never put the girl I love in custody beside me. I think that is a most unmanly thing.

Eiji [*laughing sardonically*]: You can chop logic all right. But I believe that she loved me in spite of hating me in a way. No matter what you may say, she is still mine. She will never be yours!

Shinichi: It is impossible unless you kill her.

Eiji: I simply will kill her, then.

Shinichi: Kill Chiyoko-san? For Heaven's sake! If you kill her, you know you can't live, either.

Eiji: It's none of your business! I will live. I have some important work.

Shinichi: Do you know what a dreadful name "murderer" is? The name will never leave you, following you everywhere all through your life. Whenever you are alone, the murdered one will come back to life and make her appearance before you. And the whole world will scream out at you, "Murderer, murderer, murderer!" [*Threateningly.*] Do you hear, they will scream, "Murderer, murderer, murderer, murderer, murderer!" One who by force cuts off a life, and that the life that was young and desiring to live, must be cursed as murderer, I say, murderer, murderer!

Eiji: I don't care how much cursed I might

be. I won't give up Chiyoko to you.

Shinichi [*quietly*]: You are a murderer, eh? At last you have killed her, haven't you?

Eiji: No, that's a lie!

Shinichi: Please open the trunk, then. You can't open it, I suppose.

Eiji: I won't be taken in by such a threat.

Shinichi: Then, you won't mind if I report this to the police?

Eiji: What if she were alive?

Shinichi: I will give you everything, then.

Eiji: Your life, too?

Shinichi: If she said she couldn't live otherwise, I would give up even my life.

Eiji: Do you love Chiyoko so much?

Shinichi: I don't know why, but I can't help pitying her. It is too pitiful to have her die now.

Eiji: It will be the same if she is already dead.

Shinichi: Forgive me, Eiji; I beg of you, please let her live! Oh, I cannot let her die now!

Eiji: Don't worry. I won't kill her.

Shinichi: Thank you. I feel much better to hear that. Well, I will be seeing you later.

Eiji: If you see Chiyoko, please tell her that I am not angry with her, and please tell her to come at once.

Shinichi: That's all right. Really I don't know how to thank you. Now I can go on the road in peace.

Eiji: When are you going?

Shinichi: I must go the day after to-morrow.

[SHINICHI *exit*, EIJI *sees him off, and he enters again.*]

Eiji: I am dead tired. I have no power to think now! [*He falls down and sleeps.*]

SCENE II

[*The scene of a nightmare. A room in a gloomy tower.* EIJI *is lost in the tower.*]

Eiji [*looking around gingerly*]: I will be safe as I have come so far. [*He is about to go into the interior when the door closes by itself. He stops in surprise. There appears the word " murderer " in big letters at the door, simultaneously on the walls of the room the same word appears and disappears here and there. Presently all these disappear.*] At last I've become a murderer. In my history, the brand of murderer is pressed hard, and not by any means can I take it off! Ah, look, my hand is blood-stained! No, it couldn't be! Ah, here is some water! [*Washes his hand in great haste.*] It won't come off, it won't come off! It becomes all the more clear! Oh, God, merciful

God, forgive me, pray take this blood off my hand! [*He washes his hands and takes them to the light in confusion. They become redder and redder; he washes them as if he is going crazy. At first it was only one hand that was red, but now both hands become red.*] Pray forgive me! Pray forgive me! A-h, a-h, what shall I do? [*Again the word "murderer" appears and disappears; the hands become still redder; he is still more confused. There comes the voice calling "Murderer, murderer, murderer." He tries to escape, but the doors at four directions are firmly closed, there is no way to get out. He runs about the room.*] Help! help! [*At the moment a woman shows herself as she is squatting down. Noticing her presence, he watches her eerily. She is weeping. Approaching her, and in a sympathetic tone.*] What are you crying for? Is there anything so sad? [*She is crying in silence. Putting his hands to console her.*] What is the matter? What is your trouble? [*She looks up. Her face has neither eyes nor nose.*] A-h! [*He steps back.*]

Woman: Murderer! [*Laughs aloud.*] Murderer! [*Still laughs.*]

Eiji: Help! help! [*He runs about. All of sudden the door opens;* EIJI *tries to get away from there but in vain.* CHIYOKO *is standing there with a pallid face. Kneeling down before her*]: Forgive me, please forgive me!

Chiyoko: Eiji-san. At the last moment I wanted to tell you that after all I loved you, but you strangled me and wouldn't give me a chance to say what I wanted to so much.

Eiji: Forgive me! forgive me!

Chiyoko: But in spite of my wanting so much to say that I had forgiven you, you wouldn't allow me to say even a word by choking me, would you?

Eiji: Please forgive me! fogive me!

Chiyoko: Why, I will forgive you. So, come along with me. [*She puts out her hand.*]

Eiji: I won't! I won't! I don't want to die!

Chiyoko: Eiji-san. I didn't want to die, either. Now, come along with me!

Woman: Murderer, murderer! [*She laughs aloud.*]

Eiji: A-h! [*He almost falls down.* Chiyoko *tries to drag him in;* Eiji *tries to extricate himself. In the midst of the struggle, chrysanthemum and maple flowers fall.* Chiyoko *looks a bit delighted.*]

Onodera's voice [*off stage*]: Nonaka, don't give way! Nonaka, don't give way so!

[*At length he gets off her hands.*]

SCENE III

[EIJI'S *room. EIJI is discovered as he has fallen down. Enter* SHINICHI *and* ONODERA.]

Shinichi: Ah me!

Onodera: Good gracious! what happened?

Shinichi [*running up to* EIJI]: Eiji! Eiji!

Onodera: What is the matter?

Shinichi: He is all right. He is living. [EIJI *is hag-ridden.*] Well, leave him alone, and let's find the trunk now. Since Chiyoko-san didn't come either to my house or to yours, I can't but think that what I have been fearing has happened.

Onodera: I don't think so.

Shinichi: She was supposed to go to your place if anything happened. So, seeing that she is not at your house and judging from his expression a moment ago, I think my fears are well-founded.

Onodera: But he was saying that he would frighten you.

Shinichi: I heard that from Chiyoko-san. If that were a mere threat, he would be more than a genius as actor; I couldn't come near him. I can't believe that any man could play such *kiogen*. If we open the trunk, you'll see that I'm right. Let's open it.

Onodera: Suppose we find something else inside when we open it?

Shinichi: How glad I will be then! I will treat you to anything. I wanted her to live, even if I died. But most probably she won't be alive. [*He tries to open the trunk, but it sticks tight. He tries again.*] Isn't there a key somewhere?

Onodera: I think Eiji-kun has it.

Shinichi: Won't you look for it for me?

Onodera: I feel a bit uneasy.

Shinichi: If the dead body were inside, we couldn't leave it as it is. We have to do something; Eiji can't dispose of the dead body by himself. I don't want to bury his whole career in oblivion as a murderer.

Onodera: Though I feel somewhat cheap, I will look for it. By the way, won't you hate him if the dead body comes out?

Shinichi: I will surely hate him. I may feel a desire to take revenge on him. But I know much of my reputation. I have no courage to do vengeance. If the worst should happen, I will help him as my brother.

Onodera: I feel easy in my mind to hear that.

Shinichi: So you, too, are of my opinion? You think that the body is inside this, do you?

Onodera: Most likely it is.

Shinichi: Most likely? Do you still think there is some hope?

Onodera: Yes, still I have some hope—that

Chiyoko-san will be back at any moment.

Shinichi: Chiyoko-san will be back? I've given up such a hope a long time ago. Haven't you got the key yet?

Onodera: Here it is! He has it in his right hand.

Shinichi: He has fallen with it in his hand? It appears the case is all the more hopeless.

[EIJI *is hag-ridden.*]

Onodera: Listen to that voice. It seems to be hopeless.

Shinichi: At last what we have been afraid must have come!

Onodera [*holding the key*]: Will you open it?

Shinichi: I haven't got any courage to open it.

Onodera: Neither have I.

Shinichi: Please open it and don't talk about it.

Onodera: Anyway we must open it. I wish it could end as a laughing matter after we open it.

Shinichi: Will you please not talk as if there were any hope?

Onodera [*unlocking it with the key*]: Now I shall take off the lid.

Shinichi: Wait! For I don't want to be upset. [*He prays, his eyes shut.*] Please!

Onodera [opening it]: A-h!

Shinichi: After all, after all, it was true! A-h, a-h! To think I would ever live to see such a thing! Wretched fellow! wretched, wretched fellow! he has committed a fatal error. But I am to blame for all this. Oh, I don't know what to do. [*He cries.*] It can't be helped. But, oh, the pity of it! Indeed, this mistake is beyond all correction. I fear there is no hope that she can come back to life?

Onodera [examining her eyes and other parts of her body]: No, there's no hope. It seems to me that more than ten hours has elapsed already since she died.

Shinichi: He is a fool! he is a fool! I believed surely he wouldn't do such a foolish thing. But it can't be helped! We have got to live on. [*He worships at the corpse; he bows before it on his knees.*] Chiyoko-san, forgive me! who have been so spiritless that made you what you are! [*He cries bitterly.*]

Onodera: Well, I shall close it?

Shinichi: Please.

Onodera: What shall we do with it?

Shinichi: I will take it home.

Onodera: Is that all right?

Shinichi: Surely, it is. I have various kinds of friends, you know? Now, as for Eiji, I'll ask you

to take care of him. I will go and fetch a car.
[*He goes out.*]

Onodera: A-h, a-h, a-h, a thing like this
seems to have happened once in a former world.
But it is most improbable in this age. Chiyoko-
san, Chiyoko-san! Please forgive them all, and
also forgive us who couldn't do anything for you.
[EIJI *is again hag-ridden.*] Eiji-kun! Eiji-kun!

[*He touches his head, and he goes out and gets a
quilt in surprise, and covers him with it, and brings
in some water to cool his head.* SHINICHI *enters with
chrysanthemum flowers and maple tree branches with
crimson foliage; opening the trunk in silence, he
buries the body with the flowers and leaves, prays
in silence, closes the lid, and locks it with the key.*]

Shinichi: Well, boys, come and lend a hand.
[*Two men enter.*]

Man: It's this trunk.
[*They carry it away in silence.*]

Shinichi: Has he a fever?

Onodera: Yes, it seems to be very high.

Shinichi: Well then, I will call up the
doctor on the phone, as there is one reliable doctor
among my friends. He is a man whom we can
take into our complete confidence. Though my
brother is a big fool, I should like to have him
live. Please take good care of him.

Onodera: I will as much as I can.

Shinichi: I am glad to hear that. Now, I will take my leave.

[*They bow to each other politely.* SHINICHI *exit.*]

[EIJI *is hag-ridden.*]

Onodera: Don't give way, don't give way, don't give way so!

Eiji [*half wakening with difficulty*]: Ah, Onodera, you have come for me? [*Notices that the trunk is gone.*] The trunk? what's become of it?

Onodera: Your brother took it away as he is going to fix everything for you. Make yourself easy about the body.

Eiji: You know everything?   [ONODERA *nods.*] Yet don't you desert me?

Onodera: None the less I won't. [*They look into each other's face.*]

Eiji: Thank you, my friend.

[*He bursts into tears.*]

— *Curtain* —